MINISTERS OF THE GOSPEL

Carlo Maria Martini
Archbishop of Milan

MINISTERS
OF THE GOSPEL

Meditations on St Luke's Gospel

Translated by Susan Leslie

 St Paul Publications

Original title: *L'Evangelizzatore in San Luca*. Copyright © 1981
Editrice Ancora, Milano, Italy.

St Paul Publications
Middlegreen, Slough SL3 6BT, England

English translation copyright © 1983 St Paul Publications
First published in Great Britain January 1983
Printed by the Society of St Paul, Slough
ISBN 085439 220 3

St Paul Publications is an activity of the priests
and brothers of the Society of St Paul who promote
the christian message through the mass media

Contents

Foreword

How, according to St Luke's Gospel, does a man become an evangelist? This is the question which this book sets out to answer.

Archbishop Carlo Maria Martini originally composed these meditations for a clergy retreat in the Archdiocese of Milan. As such, they are addressed primarily to priests, ministers of the Gospel. However their message, which is powerful, clear and above all full of hope, surely deserves a wider audience. The Archbishop's words speak not only to an 'inner circle' of clergy but to every Christian who is seriously striving to witness to the living Word of God. Perhaps, in fact, most serious Christians tend to strive too hard, imagining that all the responsibility rests with them. Archbishop Martini gently explains how, following Peter and the Apostles, we can come to a calm and loving reliance on God's power which is manifested precisely in our weakness and even through our failures.

With Archbishop Martini as our guide, we consider how Christ educates his evangelists — and we are all evangelists whether or not we are members of the ordained ministry. As the author says, "The Lord who calls us to evangelize does not call us to say or do something but above all to be something". We are encouraged to confront the living Word in the Scriptures and to apply it to our own personal situation. Archbishop Martini leaves us plenty of 'space' in which to do this. He does not press us with questions or force conclusions on us; rather he leads us to ask with him: how did Peter feel in such and such a situation? How did the Lord himself feel? From this comes our spontaneous reaction, in the form of a question: what is the Lord saying to *me* in this Gospel passage? How does he want *me* to respond? How, in the author's own words, can we "progress from having the Gospel merely on our lips to having it in our hearts. . ."?

We know that the Gospel is ever new and speaks afresh to each generation. Nevertheless, Archbishop Martini's insights are sometimes astonishingly original. He helps us to consider, for example, 'Jesus the failed evangelist', Jesus the one who 'reverses human situations'. In profoundly moving passages, he throws fresh light on the episode of the repentant Magdalen, on Peter's hour of denial, on the conversion process of the penitent thief. Most impressive of all, perhaps, is his treatment of Mary. We are so used to thinking of Mary as Mother of God and Queen of Heaven that sometimes we tend to forget that, like us, she had to make a 'pilgrimage of faith'. Starting from this quotation from *Lumen Gentium*, Archbishop Martini points out some of the stages of Mary's pilgrimage towards Calvary where she made the final and most profound surrender of her Son only to receive in return the gift of renewed and redeemed humanity.

In simple and straightforward language, Archbishop Martini helps us to take a fresh look at the Gospel and inspires us to apply its message of renewal and healing to our own lives. He takes a new look at the sacrament of penance, too, and describes in some detail the 'penitential dialogue'. He never imposes his ideas but humbly offers for our consideration the insights which he has found useful.

Archbishop Martini is a well-known Biblical scholar and his touch is firm and masterly as he relates different parts of the Gospel to each other and to the Acts of the Apostles. He does not, however, burden us with elaborate exegesis. All is clear and concise and, above all, illuminating and inspiring.

Behind these meditations we can glimpse a man who loves his God and loves his flock, a man whose heart evidently 'burns within him' as he listens to and relays the living Word of God to others.

It was Newman who said: "Those only can preach the truth duly who feel it personally; those only transmit it fully from God to man, who have in the transmission made it their own". Surely Archbishop Martini would endorse these words and encourage us to do the same.

S.L.

Towards an understanding of the kerygma

Opening Prayer

We thank you, Lord, for this time which you have given us to listen to your Word.

We ask you, Lord, to help us to listen attentively, for in your Word lies the secret of our life and identity, the key to the very realities to which you are calling us.

Take from us, Lord, all prejudice and impediment, all preconceived ideas which would prevent us from opening our hearts to your Gospel Word. Who but you, Lord, is worthy to proclaim this Word? Which of us could adequately interpret this Word of salvation?

For myself, also, as I prepare to expound your Word, I ask that you would take from me all prejudice and personal ideas so that I may show forth only what you, in the Spirit, wish to say to each one of us.

Mary, Mother of the Lord, who pondered in your heart all the sayings and doings of Jesus, help us to imitate your simplicity, tranquility and peace; take from us all strain, anxiety and nervousness and help us to listen attentively so that we may bring forth the fruit of the Gospel.

We ask you this, Mother, through your Son who so gloriously lives and reigns in our midst, in our community, in the Church throughout the ages, in the world and in history, for ever and ever. Amen.

Evangelists and pastors

How, according to Luke's Gospel, does a man become an evangelist? First of all it is necessary to explain what is meant by an evangelist and then to explain why Luke is peculiarly fitted to answer this question.

1. What is meant by an evangelist?

By the term 'evangelist' I refer to that special gift which helps towards the building up of the Body of Christ; it is mentioned in Ephesians 4:11 where Paul is speaking about the gifts of the ascended Christ. These gifts make some men apostles, others prophets, others evangelists, pastors or teachers. St Paul lists five gifts which serve to build up the Christian community which is to be the Body of Christ. We know that they are not the only gifts because in Paul's other letters we find mention of other charisms; in this verse of Ephesians, however, the Apostle is thinking specifically of the building up of the Church. The *apostle* lays the first foundation and supports the community, the *prophet* interprets God's will for the community in the present, the *evangelist* proclaims the kerygma, the Good News, and thereby adds to the community new believers, attracted by the word of salvation, the *pastor* cares for the flock which has come into being and leads it forward, the *teacher* by means of catechesis, doctrine and theology, nourishes the community spiritually. So there are five great charisms needed to form the community. A healthy and soundly based community will develop all these charisms which have been expressed in different ways in the history of the Church; the founders of communities, that is the apostles and prophets who interpreted the word of salvation in their own day, passed on their tasks to other ecclesiastical officers and functionaries, and now it is the bishops' job to keep the community together and to interpret God's will in the present day. It is the bishop's function to teach and unify.

The next two charisms, evangelists and pastors, although pertaining to the bishop as well, refer in particular to those who have the specific charge of the various members and positions in the community. For the most part in fact these days the Church entrusts her priests with the double task of evangelist and pastor; above all the task of evangelist is not — as the New Testament indicates — left exclusively to the hierarchy and can be extended, under their direction, to laypeople, which is happening today.

However, the main work and fundamental responsibility of evangelization and pastoral care is divided between bishops and clergy, and the clergy are responsible for individual places and communities. The living Church exercises these two gifts of evangelization and pastoral care, maintaining a balance which will naturally vary according to situations and circumstances. When the balance is lost and a church for example becomes purely evangelistic without taking care to sustain and guide the community, then we have the sort of enthusiastic church which forges ahead without building itself up. When, on the other hand, the emphasis is on pastoral care, then the church spends all its energy feeding itself and fails to expand — and it is expansion which *makes* it a church. So it is important for the charisms of evangelist and pastor to be used in conjunction with one another.

In a certain sense, evangelists excel in initiative, push and drive, in the ability to face different situations and to accept people of diverse opinions, to interpret the needs of those who seem far off, to enter into and make explicit the deep desire for truth, for justice, for God, which lies in every man. The evangelist does not wait for people to come to him; he goes out to meet them; he moves towards them instead of being a tower of strength to which they have to come.

This sort of evangelistic activity is described here and there in the New Testament but it appears most clearly in the figure of Philip.

Philip is the evangelist and represents this approach. In Acts 8 : 40 he evangelizes the various towns, going from one to the other; first he is beside the Ethiopian eunuch's chariot and then we find him again in another part of Palestine ministering to fresh needs. Philip makes bold to address the man who sits reading in his chariot and, without waiting to be asked, he makes the eunuch ask *him* a question and then goes on to explain the inner meaning of the text. Thereafter he is called an evangelist, one who has this gift of *euangelistes* (Ephesians 4 : 11). Acts 21 : 8 refers to "Philip the evangelist" and Acts 8 : 40 had described his activity thus: "Philip went about evangelizing all the cities". This gives us a concrete idea of this type of charism which confers a certain capacity to enter into the souls of others, to discover their unexpressed needs, to move into situations apparently far removed from the sphere of the Gospel, to help others towards conversion by detecting the first stirrings of grace, etc.

As we have seen, this is not the only ecclesiastical activity; pastoral care will always be a basic need of the Church, too. However, it is a very important charism and it may be found in differing degrees in the Church; some have it in greater measure, some smaller; some are primarily pastors, others evangelists. The Church requires her priests to have a mixture of both; or, rather, in the body of the Church both gifts are necessary to ensure balance without excessive immobility and to prevent mere enthusiasm without solid construction work.

2. How does St Luke's Gospel in particular throw light on the figure of the evangelist?

As this is not an exegetical study, we shall pause only briefly on this point. In a doctoral thesis written at the Pontifical Biblical Institute, an American student has treated this subject in some depth and has shown how all the characteristic Lucan passages — the sort of sayings of Jesus which Luke likes to group together, the particular emphases of his Gospel — most likely come down to us from the groups of evangelists who toured Palestine and Syria (Luke was almost certainly one of them). These men were particularly concerned with clarifying in their own minds the evangelistic ministry in which they were engaged. This was 'their' problem, hence their choice of material from the records of Jesus' life, their selection of his words and the order in which they presented them.

For this very reason Luke felt the need to continue with Acts in order to give a series of examples of evangelization and to follow the Gospel — which gives particular emphasis to Jesus' evangelistic power and his training of evangelists — with a second volume in which there were concrete examples of evangelization in the early Church.

So the Gospel according to St Luke is the best model for our own evangelistic activity. Here we can recall for example that Luke alone mentions the famous 70 or 72 who are those same itinerant evangelists whose main aim was to go round proclaiming the Word, and who were certainly in existence after the lifetime of Jesus. Afterwards they continued this type of activity, thus helping to build up the collections of words and sayings of Jesus which appear above all in the second part of the Gospel in several characteristic episodes, some of which we shall be considering later on.

How shall we approach this Gospel and what method do we need in order to answer the question: how is the evangelist formed in the school of Jesus? I have in mind a method which should help to bring our attention to various focal points of the Gospel which seem to me typically Lucan and specially helpful to us as we reflect on our task as evangelists. As a starting-point let us take two scenes which, seen together, form a framework for the Gospel.

The first is the opening scene: *Jesus at Nazareth*: Luke 4:16-30. This is a typically Lucan narrative constructed from various materials of the evangelical tradition — they can be found here and there in the other Gospels. Luke puts them together to give an introductory scene for his presentation of the Gospel story.

The second focal scene is that of *Emmaus*: Luke 24:13-35. This is also peculiar to Luke who has elaborated it with a view to showing us Jesus as a master of evangelism.

Let us then enter the *school of the Gospel*. We do this by entering into the glorious manifestation of God in the hiddenness of Christ's poverty. God can transform us as we enter into the power of Jesus' life recorded in the words of the Gospel and still alive today by the power of the Holy Spirit.

Jesus the failed evangelist

First scene: Luke 4:16-30

Jesus goes to Nazareth and enters the synagogue; the scroll is given to him and he opens it and reads a passage from Isaiah: "The Spirit of the Lord rests upon me. . ."; then he rolls up the scroll and sits down while all the people watch him intently. Luke emphasizes the fact that this is a

13

decisive moment in Jesus' life. If he makes a mistake now perhaps his whole ministry will go wrong. This is the moment of first impact; if a man starts off badly there may be serious consequences. There is an air of rather tense expectancy: let us see what he has to say, this man everyone is talking about! So they all watch him closely and when Jesus speaks, according to St Luke's account, he says in effect just one thing: "See, this scripture has been fulfilled". At this point it is not clear what exactly is happening; to this day exegetes have not succeeded in unravelling the mystery of verses 22 and 23. At first the people seem pleased and then they begin to ask: who is he, what is he doing, why didn't he do those miracles here. . . ? In fact the first apparently favourable impression quickly fades. Jesus senses that the atmosphere is becoming hostile and starts speaking again: "You will surely quote me this proverb: Doctor, heal yourself — Do here in your own town what we have heard you did in Capernaum!" Then he adds: "No prophet is well received in his home town. Let me tell you, there were plenty of widows in Israel in Elijah's time when there was a drought for three and a half years and there was a great famine throughout the land; but Elijah was sent to none of them but to a widow of Sarepta in Sidon. There were plenty of lepers in the time of Elisha the prophet but none of them was healed but Naaman the Syrian".

At this juncture the crowd's emotions erupt and the meeting breaks up in anger: Jesus is hounded out at once to be killed and it looks as if his last hour has come; in a single day everything seems to be over; his ministry has failed. This is where our meditation begins.

I must admit that each time I look at this passage I find myself wondering: now why did Luke begin his Gospel like that? And I think that had I wanted to write a gospel as a guide to evangelists, I would have taken a series of beautiful and attractive scenes which showed Jesus as a successful evangelist, the sort of man one would want to follow; I would have produced a thoroughly positive series of pictures of Jesus' methods, his ability to understand,

14

persuade and motivate people, and only after a few chapters would I have drawn attention to the difficulties and problems.

I am constantly amazed that Luke should have started his account of Jesus' public ministry with a scene which could be entitled: *Jesus the failed evangelist.*

Jesus did not succeed, he failed to make himself heard and understood and he had to depart in haste. I am struck afresh by this each time I read this Gospel and I say to myself: How would I have written this scene? Why does the Gospel present Jesus in such a strange way? Let us reflect on this: Jesus the failed evangelist. For this example of evangelistic failure seems almost to be given to us as an example to follow.

Rather than attempt a quick answer to these questions, let us ponder this very real problem: why did Luke present the start of Jesus' ministry like this? Let us reflect on several points, starting at the last verse, verse 30: "Jesus, going through the crowd, went on his way". Think of the deep sadness of Jesus' departure: it is clear that we have here an example of the mysterious power of God. Jesus was not killed and for some unknown reason he was allowed to leave; perhaps at the last moment the crowd took fright at what they were doing, they were afraid of their own reaction and so Jesus was able to go away. But how did he feel as he left that place? Surely he went away feeling defeated.

This is the first picture of Jesus the evangelist that is presented to us: defeated, hunted, unheeded, unwelcome, and it is indeed a mysterious scene if we consider that Jesus *is* the Evangelist. We can also imagine the suffering, for example, of Mary his Mother at seeing her Son has failed, the suffering of his friends and admirers who do not understand what has happened, who fear what might happen next and who believe that their fondly nourished hopes have been in vain.

Having formed a clear picture of this scene in our minds, let us now look for similar scenes in the New Testament; this is not the only scene of its kind and if Luke has put it here it is because it serves to illustrate a constant element of the Kingdom of God. Here are two examples.

The first seeks to interpret this passage of Luke's Gospel in the light of the Acts. The situation and the feelings of Jesus when he has to go away can be found for example in Acts 13:45, when, after an apparent success at Antioch in Pisidia, Paul and Barnabas return to preach: "The Jews were filled with jealousy and contradicted everything Paul said, blaspheming". So they had to leave, just as Jesus had to leave. Their ministry was unsuccessful, the Word was not accepted. From here we can go on to examine other pages of the New Testament where the suffering of the evangelist is not hidden from us. Jesus, who says "I will make you fishers of men", does not deceive his hearers by adding: "and they will all turn out well, you will catch a lot at once". Although it is true that we do not know Jesus' feelings at the moment when he was chased out of Nazareth, we do know Paul's feelings in similar situations: "We do not want you to be unaware, brothers, of the tribulation we underwent in Asia when we were bowed down beyond our strength" (2 Corinthians 1:8). Those are strong words of Paul's: "beyond our strength"; that is, all that has happened has upset us, we can't go on, "we even despaired of our lives", we were at the point of saying: it's all over. Like Jesus at Nazareth, it looked as if all their activities would be over in a few hours' time. "We had even as it were received a death sentence in order to teach us not to rely on ourselves but on the God who raises the dead" (2 Corinthians 1:9). Again in Acts 14:22 the disciples are taught that "through much tribulation we must enter the Kingdom of God".

So Paul experienced several times, in these sad departures of his from one city to another, what Jesus experienced in that first scene. It could be pointed out that that first scene was constructed by Luke and it is true, but that only serves to aggravate the problem of why Luke wrote that part of his Gospel in such a way. The answer is that Luke wanted us to think deeply, from the very start, on the true nature of the evangelist.

Turning back to Luke 4:16-30, let us look at a very striking element in the composition which can be observed in the words: "All eyes in the synagogue were fixed on him" (Luke 4:20) and the words: "You will say to me: Doctor, heal yourself" (4:23), "but no prophet is well received in his home town and Elijah and Elisha did many miracles outside Israel" (cf. 4:27). How is the figure of Jesus the evangelist presented to us in these two instances, when the people fix their eyes on him and when he confronts the people's anger?

In the first scene we can observe a fairly common phenomenon: the people are expecting a lot of Jesus, they are almost trying to take him captive, they are all there to hear him and they are trying to make him live up to *their* expectations. These are the expectations of a confined setting such as Nazareth — the expectations of the labourer or tradesman. Looking at these expectations in the light of the story of the early Church, of the arguments among Jesus' disciples as to who was the greatest, of the tension between Jerusalem and Galilee, one can already glimpse a certain eagerness to 'appropriate' the prophet, to make him an object of local pride, and even of local profit: after all, if he starts performing a few miracles, we are in charge of the inns, we can make a bit on the side. We need to take into account these very realistic aspects of the mentality of the early Church: "the prophet belongs to us"; people are a bit annoyed because he did not start there, but in Capernaum; do here what you did in Capernaum, you are one of us, we have helped you on your way and now you owe us something in return. . . .

On the one hand, Jesus is threatened by being imprisoned by other people's expectations of him, by an attempt to align what he says with their hopes and needs; they want him to be a success which means that they want to entrap him in the web of petty concerns which go to make up the social fabric of a small town.

On the other hand, however, one can see the extreme liberty exercised by Jesus. He speaks quite freely because he cares nothing for success or personal gain or for the bad reputation which this first encounter could win for him in the surrounding villages, or for the people who will not want him any more and will no longer invite him to their

17

homes. Instead he even seems to be provoking the people a bit by reminding them that there are other frontiers, other horizons and other much wider interests in the Kingdom of God; he reminds them that the pagans are worth more than this village, because they have been judged worthy of God's special presence.

Jesus appears here as the evangelist gifted with complete liberty of spirit, a liberty so profound that it encompasses the mystery of God in the whole world.

This liberty gives him, right from the start, a prophetic stature quite beyond that of a small country preacher; it is the stature of a man whose free vision encompasses the whole world, a man who has before his eyes the horizons of God himself.

Called to be with Jesus

What is the Lord teaching us in this our first encounter with his evangelistic methods? He is teaching us that to evangelize does not mean primarily doing something, getting a certain result, putting a stone in place, but it means partaking of Christ's freedom and breadth of vision; it means entering into the richness of this extraordinary liberty.

Obviously this does not mean that we should imitate Jesus by being provocative — now and then we fall into that through bad temper or pique! — but it means we should imitate the complete detachment with which he could preach the liberty of God. If we go back to the beginning of the passage, we shall see that Jesus is preaching liberty, liberation, a new way of life, the habitual presence of the Kingdom which sets men free (Luke 4 : 18-19). But he could do this because he was already living in this absolute liberty, quite unaffected by the immediate, restricted expectations of the people; he is the one who, in his person, proclaims the presence of the Lord's Anointed who liberates, enlightens, illuminates and grants remission of sins. *The liberating message which Jesus brings is himself.*

What is most striking in this first part of the scene is

the extreme personalization of the message, it is more a sermon on the messenger than on the message: "The Spirit of God rests upon me, for he has anointed *me*, he has sent *me*". From all the Old Testament passages which he could have chosen, he selected one which gives an extremely personalized image of the Messiah, "He has sent *me* to set free, to forgive, to proclaim".

The first thing we should understand from this very rich Gospel passage is this: the Lord who calls us to evangelize does not call us to say or do something, but above all to be something; to be with him and share his liberty and his mission. His liberty comes from being the Son, at one with the Father. That is the first message embodied by Christ: man is set free by sharing in the life of Jesus the Son, the one who proclaims the Gospel of liberation. We should ponder deeply on this because it lies at the very heart of the call to evangelize. We cannot help, liberate and calm others unless we ourselves are first of all liberated, calmed and saved by the presence of Jesus, by our abiding in him as liberator and saviour.

Finally, we may well ask how it was that the people of Nazareth failed to listen to him.

They failed to listen, probably, because what he had to say was to their disadvantage, their hopes were disappointed. We might well examine our own consciences and ask: what personal disadvantage, what disappointed hopes could prevent me from accepting Jesus as liberator and saviour, as a messenger of Good News for *me?*

So let us open our hearts in prayer as we listen to the Word, to the salvation which Jesus promises, above all, to the evangelist.

Difficulties in understanding the kerygma

Second scene: Luke 24:13-55

Let us now take the second episode, which stands in contrast to the first and which is also one of the focal points in the construction of Luke's Gospel: the account of the two disciples of Emmaus: Luke 24:13-35. Here we can consider 'Jesus the successful evangelist', thus drawing a parallel between the first and last scenes of the Gospel.

Let us bear in mind a few of the questions raised by the last meditation on the Jesus who was not well received at Nazareth. Nazareth appears at first sight to provide a perfect setting for 'spiritual exercises': a top preacher, a ready audience, tuned-in to the speaker and having a common language. But it is a failure. We have tried to look at the innermost thoughts of the Nazarenes and to compare them with our own inner attitudes; in fact there is something more for us to understand here.

The Gospel reveals the kerygma to us and it is our difficult task to handle the kerygma, not as a cudgel to beat men's backs but rather as the two-edged sword of Scripture which strikes home, going precisely where it is needed. We must take care to recognize the true kerygma as distinct from all the other things which *appear* to be evangelical truths but are in fact nothing but fakes, imitations and approximations and so give rise to difficulties and uneasiness.

In fact the people of Nazareth did not hear the kerygma at all: they heard an imitation or approximation, highly coloured by their own attitudes; they did not really open themselves to the words of Jesus.

To pursue this theme, let us now look at the Emmaus story section by section, with regard to several points.

First of all, let us take a close look at these two disciples: *who are they*, whom do they represent, what do they experience as they go on the road to Emmaus?

Next we will look at Jesus: what is Jesus doing to them, how does he behave?

Thirdly, we shall ask ourselves: *what is the reaction* of the two disciples when Jesus approaches them?

Finally, we shall ask what Jesus proposes to them and what is *the result of that proposal*. Each word has a profound significance because behind it lies the conversion experience and reception of the kerygma by the primitive Christian community; this experience is worth pondering even in terms of linguistic expression. It is a case in which the words are not stones but diamonds which need to be polished if they are to shine brightly enough to illuminate our path.

The crisis of the evangelist

Let us take these points in turn.

1. *Who are the two disciples?* "Now two of the disciples were on their way that day to Emmaus, a village some seven miles from Jerusalem." So they are two of *them,* two *ex auton* — the Greek tells us — two of the privileged group; they are not two casual disciples: they are people whom we would count as 'ours', that is, the sort of people we could cultivate and follow, in whom we would place certain hopes, in fact, two rather special members of the primitive community. And they go on their way — this becomes increasingly apparent — at a time of crisis and disillusionment: what made him do it? what can we hope for now? we were mistaken, nothing is happening, words are no good to us anymore, what we were hoping for has not happened. . . They are going through a time of crisis which is one of the normal trials of the evangelist and they are going through it by way of example to the whole community; and they do so, not by denying anything but by simply going on with their own pursuits, taking up more concrete and immediate occupations, everyday tasks, perhaps, such as cultivating their fields or visiting friends; the sort of things, in fact, which give satisfaction. Their expectations of the kerygma have grown vague and confused. The text makes it quite clear: "they were talking about everything that had hap-

pened" (24:14) and "they were arguing together" (v. 15); and, further on, "they stopped sadly".

How then shall we see these people? The abandonment of the kerygma has brought them no joy; they have not resigned themselves, saying: All right, it was an experience which ended badly. They still feel this experience bitterly; so they discuss and argue as to whose fault it was, they blame their own lack of prudence. As always happens when things go wrong and people look for someone to blame, someone will point out that he has made a mistake in order to dispel the sense of bitterness and discontent.

That verb *syzetein* — "they were arguing" — occurs again in Acts 15:7, 10, where mention is made of the violent arguments in the early Church about circumcision. We can see that, even though they had chosen to walk together, despite a certain friendship between them, there was also division; something had happened to upset them and they could not agree over it or find any peace. We ourselves can think of all the times when we — who have invested a lot of energy in evangelism, in fact have staked our whole lives on it — can recall how upset we get when something goes wrong and even if we perhaps try to rise above it and put it out of our minds, in fact our hearts remain bitter and guilty because we feel we have failed in the very things we believed in most.

Priests in particular should not be ashamed of being vulnerable in this way. They have really given their lives to the service of God and the Church and to evangelism: if they were unaware or indifferent, they would recover quickly enough, which would indicate that the whole venture did not mean very much to them. The failure to achieve what we set out to do, the disappointment of our hopes, these do harm and tend to create unhappiness, quarrels, even mutual accusations and the various divisions which result from them. All these things show that the work of evangelism, instead of bringing us peace, has brought us disquiet, fatigue, uneasiness; this should give rise to fresh questions.

2. The second point. *What is Jesus doing?* Here we really start a deeper acquaintance with the Lord who is

both the Good News and the bringer of good news, or evangelist.

What tactics does Jesus use? Let us read carefully: "Jesus drew near and started to walk with them". There is powerful symbolism in this very brief sentence. While they were in a state of confusion and bitterness, Jesus approached them, so it is he, as an evangelist, who takes the initiative of salvation. Once again it is Yahweh, the God of mercy, who draws near to man in his confusion, to the evangelist in difficulties who needs to be evangelized himself! "Jesus drew near and started to walk with them".

What a telling detail! *He starts to walk with them,* at their pace, for quite a while without saying anything. Thus he bears them company, he is accepted as an unknown travelling companion, discreet, unobtrusive, someone who does not make them lower their voices and speak in undertones. They go on talking because Jesus seems friendly and they quite naturally include him in the conversation. At a certain point, however, Jesus asks a question: "What is all this you are talking about?"

He could have intervened, coming as he did straight from the glory of God, by describing that glory in the midst of mankind and in that way he could have enlightened and cured them in a moment.

Instead, he uses another method: the progressive method of questioning, urging them to bring out their problem gradually.

Here we see Jesus, the wise teacher of evangelism helping the two to *help themselves;* he does not upset them with his prophetic intuition, telling them that they are mistaken but he helps them to clarify their own thoughts and to realize what they are doing so that they can sort out their interior confusion by seeing it objectively.

Jesus asks the right question; it often happens in such cases that someone forces the issue, perhaps by being untruthful, trying to distract others or changing the subject. But this sort of thing often leads to a closing of the discussion; if sometimes this is just as well because the argument itself is trivial, at other times it is certainly a mistake. In this case, Jesus realizes that the point at issue is a profound one and he questions them on their *topic of conversation* and also on their *state of soul*: "Why are you sad?" or, according to some translations, "They stopped sadly". These words immediately bring out the sadness which lies at the heart of the situation and the two disciples can no longer evade the simple, human question of Jesus.

What is the answer? The answer is in two parts. At first it is slightly impertinent, almost irrelevant: "Are you the only stranger who doesn't know about all this?" And Jesus, as if nothing had happened, ignores this initial brusqueness, knowing that the immediate response is often not the true one but is merely a withdrawal into one's shell to avoid the sudden exposure of one's deepest self. Jesus accepts the discourtesy and neutralizes it by his patience and goodness and takes up the thread of the conversation again.

Only half the kerygma

Now comes the second part of the story of the 'two depressed disciples' and it comes in the form of a truly surprising reply to Jesus' question. (Luke composed this passage with masterly humour.) If, in fact, we examine all the words in their answer to Jesus' question, even in their language structure, we will realize that the two disciples are reciting the kerygma, saying the words of the Creed, the very words used to proclaim Jesus of Nazareth.

If we compare them with Peter's preaching of the kerygma in Acts 2; 3; 10, and with Paul's in Acts 13, we can see that they echo the same words: "Jesus of Nazareth, a prophet powerful in word and deed before God and the people". This is the message of salvation which Peter is to proclaim solemnly at Jerusalem: "and this prophet powerful in word and deed was handed over by the chief priests and our rulers condemned him to death and killed him". These are the words of the kerygma which will be preached as the message of salvation in the early Church.

This is the *message*. This is the 'comical' situation described by Luke: these men are announcing the message of salvation as if it were a misfortune; they are proclaiming the message in tones of dismay. The word *skythropoi* (v. 17)

24

which describes their faces is a term which can also be found in Matthew 6:16 where Jesus says: "When you fast, do not make long faces", and the faces of the two disciples were positively funereal! Luke plays subtly with these contrasting elements: these men have the words of the kerygma on their lips but they do not understand them as such and so they proclaim them as if it were a dreadful and irreparable disaster. And then they go on to say: "We were hoping that he would be the one to liberate Israel but now it is three days since all this happened; some women frightened us — they went at once to the grave and did not find the body but saw some angels who said he was alive" (v. 21). Here the kerygma, although in less obvious form — it is not the *outos egerthe* ("he is risen indeed") — still contains its basic elements: the three days, the women at the tomb, the angels, the news that he is alive. But it is related here as something quite incomprehensible, something which should not have happened and which is a tragedy for all those who had set their hopes on him. This is what I call 'only half the kerygma'; the words are there but the heart is not, rather the heart is full of sorrow, resignation and disappointment which embitters those who say the words and fails to convince those who hear them.

When Jesus is faced with this living contradiction, what does he do? First let us think for a moment how we would have reacted to a similar situation: a dramatic situation where people are afflicted by an incurable disease which weighs on their minds so that they must always be talking about it; a situation where families are victims of a disaster, or where the mentally ill are unable to overcome their personal tragedy or vice. Or again there is the situation of the unemployed who are not in a position to find work, a situation which is in fact partly avoidable but which perhaps people do not succeed in avoiding — how in fact is one going to react to that? Sometimes we take the course of reducing the facts to a minimum, refusing to accept the burden of evil which the other person sees, cutting it down to more manageable proportions; or else we take the line of encouragement: be brave, we'll be on hand, we'll pray — and even we ourselves sense the inadequacy of what we are saying. Sometimes we try compassion, showing that we are seeking to stand by them and understand them. These are the various ways in which we might have tried to help the two disciples from Emmaus. But I believe none of our answers would have had the courage to be the same as Jesus' answer, which is the answer of the true kerygma, the word of salvation which proceeds from the God of truth.

The whole kerygma

How does this word of salvation come? It is really new, unexpected, incredible, utterly simple, perfectly adapted to the situation because it tackles the problem squarely from the inside. It is exactly the answer we would like to have in the situations I have just described, so that we could break through the evil inherent in them all. Jesus answers in three ways:

First of all, he attacks, with a sharp admonition: "You fools, how slow you are to believe all that the prophets said!" This remark must have brought them up with a jolt: how was it that this man, who had been so peaceable, friendly and humble up until then, had suddenly turned so aggressive? And yet, when someone is so mistaken about the kerygma and has so entirely misunderstood the true values of the Kingdom, it is necessary to give him a jolt and bring him to a realization of man's true position, making an appeal both to his intelligence and his responsibility. In fact there is nothing more humiliating than being told: you have been neither responsible nor intelligent. Jesus shows how the state of bitterness and religious confusion — for we are dealing with religion here — demands a radical change, a change even of doctrinal view-point. "Foolish and dull-witted men", you think you have been in the school of Jesus and you have learned nothing! All your exercises have been useless.

Secondly, Jesus shows how the Bible had pointed to the drama of salvation: "Should not the Christ have suffered all this before entering into glory?" Jesus produces a key to the understanding of the recent events; the events remain the same but the key gives them a completely different meaning.

What was, after all, the big problem for these men? The same problem we all have each time we face the sort of situation which seems to us to undermine all our values and finally to destroy the Righteous One. We say: "Where is God? Why doesn't he show himself? If this was a man of God, why didn't God help him, what has become of justice and divine power?" This is the great drama into which the evangelist enters when things do not go according to plan. This is our task every time we enter new, different and unforeseen situations, when expectations, hopes and plans are frustrated by events and we have to re-think our ideas about the will of God. The Psalmist's cry "Why are you hiding yourself, Lord? Why do you not show yourself?" is born of this agonizing need to understand why things have gone this way, why justice seems perverted and evangelical truth deprived of its power while the nonsensical and the absurd take over, and a sense of scepticism and defeatism prevails.

Jesus' answer is the only answer to the experience we are going through; it is the key to our understanding, as it reminds us of the designs of divine providence: God has everything in hand and it was his plan that they should turn out in this way; everything has gone according to the plan of salvation which Jesus now gently starts to explain. You had this plan of salvation in Scripture. You know how Abraham was put to the test and how the people thought they would be drowned while crossing the Red Sea; you know what suffering Moses and our fathers went through before entering the Promised Land; it was by means of these dark times that God formed his people. Yet you did not understand because you failed to penetrate the meaning of the Scriptures and so these events upset you. But theological understanding serves to broaden your outlook until you can perceive the unity of God's mysterious ways in the lives of men and in the world.

So Jesus acts as evangelist and *didaskalos* or teacher: he uses his gifts as exegete and catechist to provide the explanation the two disciples were looking for.

But we know that the episode does not end there. In fact when the disciples have stopped arguing and are able to be friends again — at first they had been quarrelling together and then they made it up and agreed on the spur of the moment to invite this man to supper — they sit down to table and then *Jesus makes himself known to them*. He makes himself known with the sign already familiar to them, the Breaking of the Bread, by which Luke certainly intends to indicate all the future manifestations of Jesus in his Church in the Breaking of the Bread. Jesus shows himself to be near them, present with them. This manifestation, this presence, removes all doubts and provides a thorough explanation which is expressed like this: "Didn't we feel our hearts burning while he spoke to us on the road and explained the Scriptures to us?" (v. 32). Jesus the evangelist not only announces the kerygma, proclaiming the plan of salvation by making it real in his own person, but he also makes men's hearts burn within them. This is the most striking characteristic of the whole series of Jesus' revelations of himself to them. They do not say: Jesus spoke well, he explained it well, he was a good preacher, he set us on the right path, but they said: he kindled our hearts, he revealed himself as the friend who is able to liberate our embittered hearts, embittered because, from our point of view, God's plans seemed totally unacceptable. Here we touch on a very important point.

In Bernard Lonergan's *Method in Theology* there is a passage on the power of God's love in theology. This sentence struck me particularly: "The world is too evil for us to accept unless we love". If we really face some of the things that are happening today, how can we accept the world, how can we believe in a just God?

This is the great difficulty for many people and evangelists are often asked this question: how is it possible to believe in a God who allows such things, such monstrous cruelty, such atrocities? Of course we can always explain that the fault lies with men whom God created and left free, so also leaving us at each other's mercy for good or ill. But obviously the problem will not be resolved unless — as in this case — we place ourselves in the presence of Jesus and his Spirit. Only God can open our hearts to perceive his loving plan for the world, only God can help us to give ourselves in accordance with this plan, as Christ crucified first gave himself to suffer and experience in himself all the pain and tragedy of the world.

The important thing is not a perfectly logical answer, even if we could find one; what really counts is to know oneself surrounded by the love of God and to be convinced that Jesus — who is Justice, Love and Wisdom — is alive and able to give life to all who have been crushed by injustice.

Luke's sentence: "Didn't we feel our hearts burning while he explained the Scriptures to us?", reminds us of two things:

Firstly, that we need to open up the Scriptures, to proclaim and explain them.

Secondly, that this explanation and proclamation of the Scriptures should make us feel the life-giving power of the Spirit in our own hearts, the Spirit of him who raises the dead. Those who listen to our preaching should be able to share this same hope.

The ending of the Emmaus story is too rich in meaning to be expressed in a few words: it is a story that we should feel in our hearts rather than attempt to express in logical terms and for this reason we should ask to enter into the heart of the Lord to discover what he, as true evangelist, has to say to us.

In the following meditations, we shall go on to discover how we, too, can be evangelists like Jesus; how we can progress from having the Gospel merely on our lips to having it in our hearts.

What does the kerygma do, and what exactly is it?

Let us start this meditation by asking ourselves: *what is it in my life which most prevents me from getting what I really want?*

Before continuing our reflections on how the evangelist is trained to proclaim the kerygma, it is as well to meditate on that proclamation itself. Assuming Luke's connection with Acts, I would like to take the question in two stages: first let us ask what the kerygma *does* and secondly let us ask what the kerygma *is*.

1. *What does the kerygma do?* It brings about all the things which happened at the end of the conversation of Jesus with the disciples of Emmaus (Luke 24:13-35). Things happen which change a person from the inside, giving him a new perspective and fresh inspiration.

All this is described in various ways: first, their eyes are opened (v. 31); secondly, their hearts burn within them (v. 32); thirdly, they run to tell the others (v. 33) the message which they simply cannot keep to themselves; fourthly, they find all the others gathered together and they tell them the Word.

There are many other points that could be brought out of this passage, but we have concentrated on a few here in order to illustrate the *change* which men undergo when they hear the Good News. Eyes are opened, hearts burn, there is a desire to tell others and to create community. And each one of us can develop these points either from his own or others' experience.

Where these things happen, we have a true proclamation of the Gospel; if they do not happen, we have the sadness of the two disciples on the road to Emmaus — a sense of heaviness, fear of the future, frustration; and then it means that there has been no Gospel proclamation or that it has not been properly expressed.

I draw your attention to the attitude of those two disciples because it contains a valuable lesson for the Christian life: they had everything, right from the start of their journey; they had the words of the kerygma, they had the central figure of the kerygma, Jesus, alive with them, but their eyes were not open, nor were their hearts burning and so they were not living right. They failed to see or realize or understand and the kerygma consists precisely in an opening of the eyes and the recognition that in our present situation God has revealed himself and has opened up new perspectives, quite surpassing our expectations.

The kerygma leads to an interior transformation which fills us with joy. We can imagine the whole community gathered together with the Eleven to hear the news that the Lord has indeed risen and has appeared to Simon. We seem to see that community exulting, jumping for joy, radiant.

I saw this sort of joy expressed in dancing during a recent visit to the dioceses of Africa; the people started dancing because their inner exultation could no longer be contained. Once I was invited to a pastoral council; and all the members of the council were gathered together in silence, all very serious. Then I asked them to tell me something about themselves, to speak to me about their parochial problems. One of them got up and said: "Look, we have come together in many different groups — Catholic Action, Daughters of Mary and others — but the important thing is that we should all wish each other well and that we should show it". Then he started to clap his hands and dance in the middle of the room and one after another everyone else got up and started to dance together. It was a really wonderful sight! Later, of course, there was talking and discussion, but that was how the meeting started.

The effect of the kerygma is precisely this outburst of joy, expressed outwardly; we discover it when we meet people who have reached this stage of Christian maturity.

I once knew a young man whose experience of life was far removed from the influence of the Gospel; after having made some progress and having understood the meaning of the Gospel in his life, he said to me, quite simply: it was as if I had just come alive and everything was new to me, everything seemed great and beautiful, as if I were seeing life with completely new eyes!

I remember another person who had also emerged from a very difficult situation and had made great steps in the faith; he used the very words of Acts: it was as if my eyes were opened and I saw a whole world that I had never guessed even existed. These are the effects of the kerygma.

It is the word of God, the life of the risen Christ which have entered into us and changed our lives, making us see things and situations in a new light; that light was already there so we are amazed not to have seen it before. It is rather like seeing a mountain at night and having a sense of heaviness and fear; then, when dawn breaks, we marvel at the newly discovered colours, the light on the snow. This is what the kerygma does in our lives, this is the result of receiving the Good News.

If we think about this, each of us will be able to find similar experiences, our own or others; the Lord grants these to us so that we may have a deeper understanding of what happens to a man's life when the message of salvation comes to him.

2. *What is the kerygma?* It is well to re-read the pages of Acts and the Gospel which set forth the kerygma. Luke is the evangelist of the kerygma and the whole of the third Gospel is to do with the kerygma, the message of salvation. But Luke also expresses the kerygma in briefer and more concise forms: these are the so-called missionary sermons of Acts (cf. Acts 2; 3; 10; 13). These chapters contain four great sermons which, along with other minor speeches, constitute the exposition of the Gospel message of salvation. Besides these concise and direct expositions there are others, given indirectly, where the Acts of the Apostles recounts what happens when a community is transformed by the Word; the best known of these are the accounts of communion and community life, in Acts 2:37-48 for example, where there is a description of the changes in a group of people who have really accepted the Good News.

I have stressed what, for me, are the characteristic elements of this brief proclamation of the kerygma, points which obviously can be expressed in a number of ways. But woe to us if we are content merely to repeat the kerygma, doing nothing but recite the words of the Bible! Especially in the case of the unprepared, this may not even sound right. It is very important for us to note the *structural* points of the kerygma, those which always figure, one way or another, in the message which we proclaim or speak or suggest discreetly — depending on the situation; we are aiming, after all, at enlightening men's hearts by the Gospel message; we are not only pastors of a community but also preachers of the Gospel hope to those who are without hope and who stand especially in need of the Good News.

Let us now look at one of these sermons to see the attitudes and points which seem specially noteworthy.

Peter's sermon (Acts 2:14-36): "Then Peter, standing with the Eleven, raised his voice (note that he raised his voice — for this is something that a man proclaims with his whole being because he lives it in depth, he believes it, it is no mere hypothesis) and addressed them in these words: Jews and people of Jerusalem, pay attention to what I am about to say and listen to me carefully. These men are not drunk, as you think, because it is only nine in the morning; rather, they are fulfilling the words of the prophet Joel:

In the last days — says the Lord —
I will pour out my spirit on every human being
and your sons and daughters will prophesy
and your young men will have visions
and your old men will have dreams;
truly I will pour out my spirit on my servants,
both men and women,
and they will prophesy.
I will work wonders in heaven above
and perform miracles on the earth beneath,
blood and fire and smoking vapours.
The sun will go dark and the moon
will turn into blood

33

before the coming of the day of the Lord,
that great and awesome day.
Then whoever calls on the Lord's Name will be saved.

Men of Israel, listen to this: Jesus of Nazareth was a man approved by God amongst you by the wonders, signs and miracles which God worked through him, as you well know; God's will and providence allowed him to be handed over to you; and you, by the hands of lawless and impious men, killed him by fastening him to the gallows. But God raised him up, freeing him from the pains of death: for it was impossible for him to be overcome by death. In fact David says of him:

I saw the Lord continually before me
For he is at my right hand so that I shall not stumble.
For he makes my heart glad
and my words are full of joy:
even though I die, I shall rest in hope,
for he will not abandon my soul
to the realm of the dead,
you will not allow your faithful servant
to undergo corruption.
You have shown me the paths of life,
you will fill me with joy in your presence.

Brothers, let us speak frankly. Our father David died and was buried and his grave is with us to this day. But he was a prophet and he knew that God had solemnly sworn to him that one of his descendants should occupy his throne. So, seeing into the future, he spoke of Christ's resurrection when he said that he would not be abandoned to the realm of the dead nor would his body be corrupted. This is the same Jesus whom God has raised up and we are all witnesses to this. Therefore he has been raised to the right hand of God, he has received from the Father the gift of the Holy Spirit according to the promise, and he has poured out this same Spirit which you now see and hear. David did not in fact ascend into heaven, nevertheless he says:

The Lord said to my Lord:
Sit at my right hand
until I make your
enemies your footstool.

Let the whole house of Israel then be quite sure that
God has made this same Jesus whom you crucified, both
Lord and Christ."

In the same way we can read all the other sermons,
taking note of this basic pattern of preaching. Starting from
this outline, I would like to list four elements which seem
to me particularly significant because they point to the
realities on which this communication of the Good News
is based.

The effects of the kerygma

The first point to note is a pronoun which can be found
in v. 16. The Greek is *touto estin:* that which you see is
what was said by the prophet. This is a recurrent phrase in
these sermons: "that which you see" means *"this"* —
"this" is the meaning of the experience you are having. In
chapter 3, we find: *"This* cripple who has been healed
means that God has glorified his Son".

The first characteristic of the message is the reference
to a present, live situation. The kerygma originates with a
man's actual experience, it refers to a situation through
which we are living, both I and the person to whom I speak.
This is what you are going through. This means that this
Gospel word is never something abstract: Christ has risen,
I agree: what does that mean, what does it say to me?
Christ has freed us from our sins: what has that to do with
my life? We start with an actual situation in which it is
possible to show a sign of God's power.

The sign will vary: at the Pentecost sermon it was
enthusiastic speaking in tongues by the Apostles; the sermon
in Acts chapter 3 is based on the healing of the cripple; in
Acts 10 the sermon starts with Peter's providential mission
to the house of Cornelius; the sermon in Acts 13 is Paul's

own proclamation of the Gospel as he reaches Pisidia.

So as well as the firm assurance of the preacher that the present situation of a given person can be differently interpreted to show both God's salvation and glory, there is always a link with the person who is listening. It is good news *for you, your life* can be different, *your problem* can be seen in a different light, your assessment of your situation has been mistaken, there is a way out for you; what you expect and desire to happen is this, and I can tell you that it is so.

Often the thing that links a situation to the life of the listener is quite concrete, a living Christian community, a live experience of Christianity, an experience involving the acceptance of the poor, the service of justice, love, fraternal forgiveness, communal joy. One of the impressions I retained from my African visit was that the Christian communities there showed communal joy even in their Church services which lasted for hours and were full of songs and festivity and a sense of exultation; this sort of thing draws those who are not yet Christians; these folk come to Mass because they are attracted by this new way of living, this new experience, this atmosphere of peace which pervades the whole of life — and they instinctively ask what it all means.

The second characteristic element is the presence of *God in action.* "The God of our fathers, the God of Abraham, Isaac and Jacob has glorified his Son Jesus" (Acts 3 : 13). Let us reflect for a moment on the importance of this appeal to the action of God, the active agent of the kerygma. What does this mean in the life of the person who is listening? God has your life in hand, he has not abandoned you, God is present to you, you matter to him: that is to say, we should actualize this aspect of the kerygma for each one of us.

The God of our fathers, of Abraham, Isaac and Jacob, the God of Jesus Christ, the God of St Ambrose and St Charles, the God of those who instructed me in the faith, my parents, my pastors, the God who as always in the history of my tradition, in my own life, is near me, *here* and *now*, and shows himself to *me*. It is a question, then, not only of linking oneself to the preceding tradition but also of rediscovering that the God who acted in history, who raised Jesus from the dead, who raised up the saints and those who taught us the faith, *is* 'our' God, he who is present *now* in my life by this saving action.

The third element is this: God *reverses appearances*. Let us take another look at some verses in chapter 2: "You . . . killed him by fastening him to the gallows. But God raised him up, freeing him from the pains of death".

The man who was a failure has been glorified, the one who seemed to be rejected by men has been exalted. God has reversed human appearances, he has upset man's way of looking at things by glorifying Jesus. Let us reflect on the importance of this simple statement: "God has upset human appearances and turned them upside down", for it is precisely at his point that each one of us needs to listen carefully.

Things seem to be going in such a way that we lose faith and trust and become dissatisfied and feel ourselves quite useless; we must not stop at this point, God is able to reverse the situation in your life in the same way as he reversed the situation and the human judgement of Jesus' life. Note the importance of this principle when applied to so much of St Luke's Gospel: "Blessed are the poor . . . blessed are the persecuted . . . blessed are you who weep . . .".

The Lord comes to reverse human appearances, to reverse the realities of injustice and suffering, to create new opportunities in areas of apparent failure. He comes to create a whole new world within those very situations which seem overwhelmingly dreadful to us; starting from inside me and my community, he comes to set in motion a reversal of values which will give us new hope. God's powerful intervention which raised Jesus from the dead, gives us new hope of shaping man's life: the very thing which seems hardest to you now can, by God's power, immediately become your resurrection, a path leading to undreamt of new experiences and ways of life.

The fourth element: *the person of Jesus himself* who meets you and warms your heart by the way he speaks and by the way he draws near to you in humanly perceptible form, changing your life and your way of looking at things. Above all, we should have a living knowledge of Jesus' presence with us, this being with him which enables us at certain times to relay the power of his presence to others.

The gift of the Spirit

One last point of importance: the presence of Jesus comes as a *gift*, a new interior vitality which is the *gift of the Spirit*. The kerygma, then, coming out of man's present situation, and filling that situation with God's powerful action, presents us with the God who reverses human situations by raising Jesus from the dead; he is able to reverse your life, too, *to give you an inner vitality and new power to act, which is the gift of the Spirit.*

The kerygma always leads in the end to the reality of the Spirit who changes us from within. This is expressed in various ways: with the words "the Holy Spirit which the Father has promised" or by the term *afesis amartion* or the remission of sins. What this means is, taking out of your life everything that weighs you down, crushes you and prevents you from expressing your life spontaneously and as you would wish. It means the removal from your life of those obstacles, burdens and constrictions which stop you from being yourself and make you unhappy. The power of the Spirit is that new life which transforms: it cannot be expressed in words alone, for it is the living experience of the evangelist or of the living Christian community; these are places where people can actually see the transformation wrought by faith, charity, unselfishness, patience, places where the poorest are cared for, where there is a spirit of responsibility, and courage in the face of death. These are all things which bear witness to the living presence of the Spirit.

In these matters, little things are enough, it is not necessary to do anything sensational. Perhaps we have often had this experience: a real act of charity, pardon, unselfishness, proves to be the point of entry into this new way of life. There is another way of living, thinking, loving, believing and being happy, and this other way is for you.

It is difficult to express the kerygma in words because it encompasses the whole range of redeemed man, of his encounter with God's power, with the risen Christ, and with the Spirit which is given to him.

All the same, as we meditate on the most significant points of the Gospel message, let us ask ourselves to what extent they are present in our lives rather than on our lips: to what extent do we allow ourselves to be transformed by the power of the risen Christ, by the Spirit of the God who reverses situations; do we totally entrust our lives to the God of our fathers who intervenes, not leaving us alone in our present trials and positions of responsibility but staying with us to give us life and joy?

Let us then ask the Lord truly to show us in our reading of the Scriptures and in our silent adoration all that he is for us, so that we can understand and have a really profound knowledge of the kerygma, so that it may find expression in our lives.

The sense of sin in the training of the evangelist

Let us now meditate on some episodes of Jesus' public life in which it is clearly apparent that Christ is he who reverses unhappy and hopeless human situations, and brings his disciples to a concrete realization of the nature of the kerygma and how it brings salvation.

I shall take three episodes, treating only the first in detail:

— The call of Peter: Luke 5:1-11.
— The healing of the paralytic: Luke 5:17-26.
— The pardon of the sinful woman in Simon's house: Luke 7:36-50.

The common feature of these three episodes is the sense of sin or the cleansing from sin. The evangelist must learn, above all, to convey the sense of God's merciful forgiveness of men's sins.

In chapter 4, Luke has already shown us Jesus in action: not only does he go to Nazareth as an 'evangelistic failure' but after that he courageously continues his preaching tour, he goes to Capernaum, heals a man possessed by an unclean spirit, heals many people outside the synagogue and then visits various synagogues in Galilee. Only at this point does Luke introduce Peter; first of all Jesus himself sets the example of preaching and only later does he begin to gather followers.

This is an important episode because the evangelist wants to give us a model of an *evangelist's call to the ministry:* Jesus starts his careful selection of evangelists and he does so in a way that tells them something about the sort of mission he will entrust to them and the sort of training he will give them.

"At your word I will let down the nets"

The call of Peter: Luke 5:1-11

In the background of this scene, there are a lot of people listening to Jesus. Jesus is near the lake and sees two boats; the fishermen have already got out and are washing the nets. Jesus quite freely and unhesitatingly gets into one of the boats, Peter's, just as if he were one of the family. He asks him to push it a little way from the shore and, sitting down, he begins to teach.

We can imagine the feelings of Peter who must have been proud that it was *his* boat which had been chosen: "I'm not the worst person in the village then;" — he might have said to himself — "probably Jesus understood that I'm a modest sort of chap but worthy of honour all the same . . .". This makes Peter very happy for the time being.

But there is a surprise in store for him: when the sermon is over and Peter expects to go ashore amid the congratulations of the crowd, Jesus quite abruptly tells him to push out to sea and let down the nets. Surely at that moment Peter underwent a change — the Scriptures tell us little of people's inner thoughts, leaving us to imagine them and enter into them for ourselves. From Peter's reply we can guess that doubts had arisen in his mind about the wisdom of the Master's words, for the hour is late, they have finished fishing and there are no fish.

What is more, Peter is probably thinking what fools they will look if nothing happens, he is afraid of being taken by the local people for a madman, the sort who goes out fishing at an hour when there can be no hope of a good catch. It is a difficult moment in which Peter's faith in the Master could be shaken: maybe it would be better for him simply to refuse and not take the risk of trying something which could make him look ridiculous in everyone's eyes.

We catch a glimpse of all this in the first half of his reply: "We have laboured all night and have caught nothing". This verb 'laboured' — *kopiasantes* — is a verb

41

which the New Testament uses on other occasions when describing apostolic toil. We can see our own circumstances here: I have put in a lot of work, and expended a lot of energy, I put everything I'd got into it, I've exhausted myself and nothing has come of it. There is that sense of weariness on the part of the evangelist, a certain defeatism and lack of confidence: but, Lord, you could have helped me from the start, why haven't you come until now? Here is the difficult moment in which Peter toys with various courses of action: if he gives in to this weariness, saying that he has already tried, it's no use, it's better to go home, then he will be directly refusing Jesus' offer. If, on the other hand, he decides to take a chance, to run a small risk, to ignore both his overwhelming fatigue and the threat of ridicule, if he says: "Let's jump in and get going", he will become an evangelist who has passed the test of faith: "At your word I will let down the nets". These words are of profound importance: *"epi de to remati sou": at your word,* because this is the biblical expression which indicates man's attitude to God. "I trust in your word" says the Psalmist, "It is your word which gives me life". You have afflicted me, you have permitted so much suffering, but I trust in your word.

Here Peter is no longer acting out a small private drama, he represents the man who vacillates even in simple, trivial situations which nevertheless require a certain amount of decision and courage. He stops weighing up the pros and cons and throws himself on the word of the Lord. Here we have one of the distinguishing marks which Jesus is looking for; this is the sort of minor trial with which Jesus tests and forms his evangelists.

Generally speaking, the sort of people who are very calculating, constantly preoccupied with self and with the results of what they do, who always want to check everything to see whether or not it will upset their own security, these people are poor material for vocation. In fact the true evangelist stands revealed at such moments, when it is a question of taking a little risk, throwing oneself into something, not stopping to calculate or to weigh things up too much. This irrational 'something' remains a characteristic of the evangelist: 'irrational' naturally not in the sense of being against reason but in the sense of taking some step beyond the purely secure and reliable.

To return to Peter: after all, it is he himself who takes the step out of the boat to throw himself into the lake. One needs a touch of madness to take such a step. It is that very touch of madness that makes the man. We often say — and the Pope affirmed this clearly in the encyclical *Redemptor Hominis* — that man cannot live without love: it is love which enables a man to leap into some venture, throwing all caution to the winds. Here Jesus is testing Peter to see if he has the capacity to take risks and Jesus will make him exercise this capacity more and more for it is an essential quality in an evangelist.

And when the nets are let down at Jesus' word they are filled, other boats come to help and they also are on the point of sinking. What happens then? Seeing this (here is an aspect of the kerygma: it is a fact, a remarkable and unforeseen fact), Peter discerns the manifestation of divine power and throws himself at Jesus' feet saying: "Leave me, for I am a sinful man". Something has happened. *The power of Jesus reveals Peter's sinfulness:* perhaps Peter was not among the worst sinners of Capernaum but he was certainly a man who, confronted by the power and holiness of God, sensed that there were many things in his life which were not as they should be. Indeed the most striking thing about Jesus' treatment of Peter is the delicacy which Jesus shows.

If Jesus had been the fussy sort of teacher we sometimes meet, he would have said: so you want to follow me, Peter? remember you are a sinner, so first you must truly repent of your sins and purify yourself, otherwise you will not be fit to follow me. Instead, Jesus leads Peter to make an act of faith. As a result of that act of faith, Peter realizes the greatness, goodness and power of Jesus and he easily and instinctively, without any effort, forsakes his sin. So Jesus leads Peter first of all where he wants to lead him, to sincere purification, humility, to a realization of the need of God's mercy, so that Peter will be in a position to understand the mercy of the kerygma and the word of salvation. He leads him in this totally free, human way, without hardness and upset.

We can apply this to our own way of penitence, a way which is so necessary for every man and woman in this world, and above all necessary for the evangelist. We must always remember that it is the consideration of God's mercy towards us, his power and his goodness, that helps us to realize our poverty and need of salvation. Wearisome introspection, without openness to God's power as manifested to Peter, is not only not evangelical but may even be harmful.

Now Peter can say these things quite calmly and simply, no longer fearing anyone else because of the greatness of the One who stands before him; even if the others feel he is a sinner, it no longer matters to him. By this time he has made such a decisive step in interior liberation that he has overcome all the fears which he previously had as to what other people thought and said about him.

Jesus forms the evangelist by means of these leaps of faith and by making known his divine power; gradually Christ leads him to true penitence.

The scene closes with one last surprise. Peter was expecting the Lord to confirm him in his attitude of penitence and instead Jesus says: "Have no fear; from now on, from this very moment, you will be a fisher of men".

This is a reversal of the original situation. First of all, Peter, a bit pleased with himself, has become a man capable of making a leap of faith; this trustful man was then able to acknowledge his own poverty; humbled in his poverty, he became a man full of faith. It is by such an experience of God's power that the evangelist is formed; it is the wonderful transforming power of God which works in us by reversing human situations.

The Gospel has the power of forgiveness for all who trust in it

The healing of the paralytic: Luke 5:17-26

Now let us look briefly at the second episode, the healing of the paralytic, and see what it has to teach us. What has this situation in common with Peter's situation? Here, too, five men *risk ridicule* by uncovering the roof of the house and letting the man down, without knowing if Jesus is willing to receive him; it could all have come to nothing: will he perform the miracle or not? What will happen? Will this man return home more exhausted and humiliated than before? — it is no small thing to hope for a miracle: if it doesn't happen, the man will die.

Here, too, there was an act of courage, a moment free from calculation, when these men took the first, not entirely rational step towards the Man whom they knew only slightly and yet whom they trusted completely. What happens? As a result of this act of courage and faith, the sick man's situation is completely reversed: his sins are forgiven and his illness is healed. *Jesus is seen as the one who pardons and heals:* the kerygma, the Gospel, is the power of pardon and healing for those who trust in it, who dare to take this brave step and make the leap of faith. We need courage to enable Jesus to transform us like this, we need the mature realization that only in a moment of courage, of going out of oneself, does one succeed in obtaining what one most deeply desires.

Once when I was going through the mountains I stopped to look at some marvellous waterfalls where the water fell straight down for hundreds of feet, foaming in places. This made a deep impression on me as I watched, trying to identify myself with the water and wondering: what would happen if I were afraid to throw myself down? Unlike the water, which instinctively throws itself down, I would be held back by fear, I would not take the initiative and so I would fail to be what I was meant to be.

I am what I am meant to be in the measure in which I follow that tendency to trust. It is from man's innate tendency to move beyond himself, to make an act of faith in other men, that society is born, as are friendship, love and brotherhood. If no one ever takes a risk, nothing happens. It is this trust in Jesus' word that makes salvation possible; it is a very special kind of trust that makes evangelization possible. The evangelist lets down the nets at Jesus' word, he is formed as he learns to surrender himself.

The pardon of the sinful woman in Simon's house:
Luke 7:36-50

Let us consider the central part of this episode only. What is the situation? It is rather ambiguous. Here is a man, Simon, who thinks he is important, who has the situation in hand and has taken no risks: he has received Jesus but with a minimum of courtesy because he hopes thereby to please everybody. By entertaining Jesus, he shows that he is open-minded, able to consider new ideas, a man of a certain intelligence; however, by omitting the usual courtesies, he can always say that he has held himself aloof and merely taken a look at him to hear what he had to say.

Trying to please everyone without committing oneself is precisely the kind of behaviour we are liable to fall into; yes, we do something but in such a way that no one can criticize us and so we steer carefully between two opinions without embracing either. It is true that sometimes this is necessary and circumstances demand it, but certainly the man who lives like this is not fully alive; he is behaving like Simon, who prepares a banquet for Jesus and allows the atmosphere to be tense and wary; Jesus feels he is being watched which probably prevents him from speaking easily and enthusiastically; the others are also watching one another and they, too, keep to general topics which will compromise no one.

At a certain point, a woman comes in and, breaking all the conventions, makes everyone very uncomfortable: looks are exchanged, heads turn, people make signs to one another and ask questions; everyone draws back, each blaming the others for having invited her; no one wants to admit that he knows her. Meanwhile the woman goes forward, unafraid, and in a gesture of public confession, gives Jesus those marks of affection, recognition and reverence which no one else had shown him.

That is the situation. No one present dares to take a risk; the woman on the other hand has taken a big risk: what will Jesus do, whose side will he take? Here again we can see Jesus' marvellous ability to reverse situations. Jesus will not start with a rebuke; he well knows that these crucial moments demand a certain prudence and care. By telling Simon an opportune parable and by asking a question at the end of it, he lets Simon himself know that in God's sight, and also from the point of view of human sincerity, this situation is exactly the opposite of what everyone thinks. The real intruder, the one who really should be ashamed of himself, who did not know how to behave, is Simon; the person who acted as the situation demanded, responding in a truly human way, is the woman: she is the one who understood and who grasped the reality of the situation.

Again, this is how the Gospel makes people aware of their guilt and need of purification: not by harsh rebukes which put a person on the defensive, but by giving the woman courage, resolution and liberty of heart. All this makes her a perfect type of the man or woman who seeks purification and obtains pardon from God in an act of love which transforms their whole existence.

It seems to me that these two episodes, in their different ways, throw light on what happened to Simon Peter — with his original spontaneity, loud and joyful, and then his confession of sin — again we have the reversal of a situation in which a man who publicly admits that he is a sinner, becomes a man in whom Jesus places great trust.

That is what the kerygma does: it reverses human situations and turns them round, shaming those who thought they were in control and raising up those who act in a spirit of humility, truth and simplicity, following their desire to give themselves, to do something more, to risk something for love's sake. After all the word *love*, which is not mentioned at all in the episode concerning Simon Peter, is really central: "Much has been forgiven her, for she loved much". Peter made a very loving act, as did the paralytic, quite instinctively, and both were renewed by the power of the kerygma.

The Gospel word brings man back to his own truth and spontaneity, it takes him to the place where he wants and should be by nature, that is, trustful, committed, able to take risks, to love and to express deep affection, able even to give public witness to his newly regained freedom. At the beginning of a man's formation as an evangelist it is important to stress these points. If evangelization means an inner liberation of man in the direction of his true potential, his capacity to express himself and to overcome the burden of sin, all this must be seen first of all in the evangelist himself; and Jesus, with masterly strokes, shows us how this can happen.

Our own way of penance

As we have seen, the first stage in the education of an evangelist is the true realization of God's forgiveness; we saw how swiftly Peter was moved to say "Leave me, for I am a sinful man", how the paralytic heard the words "Your sins have been forgiven" and how it was said of the sinful woman "Much has been forgiven her for she loved much".

Now let us take a closer look at our own way of penance. We know it is important — how often we have explained it to others — but we are aware, perhaps not at a very deep level, that penance is somewhat neglected in the Church today.

Frequent confession used to be normal practice as an expression of penitence; especially in some areas, this practice has been dropped to a great extent; I know towns and villages where confession has become very rare. It is replaced every now and then by penitential liturgies which after all are less demanding than the exercise of individual confession. It was not for nothing that John Paul II, in the latter part of the encyclical *Redemptor Hominis*, reminded us of the right of each of the faithful to be reconciled to God by making individual confession. This 'crisis of penance' has already been the subject of much study in the

Church today and can probably be attributed to the formalism into which the sacrament has fallen. All priests, at least the most seasoned confessors, have come across folk who made frequent confession but merely out of habit and without much benefit. . . . Now people have gone to the opposite extreme: once something has become merely habitual, people prefer to abandon it rather than go into it more deeply and make it more real.

So we are at a turning-point, uncertain of the future. The Church, however, has a much deeper sense of penitence than before, especially with regard to social sins — injustice, the lack of brotherhood, for example, — even if it is still rather indefinite in its approach to these areas. Our immediate concern, however, is with our own personal way of penance.

For Peter, as for all evangelists, there is a pressing initial invitation to penance and we must ever return to this: we have to come before the Lord with a realization of what we really are, of our own weakness and need of salvation. The risk which the Church runs — and each one of us in her — when she loses her sense of penitence, her sense of sin and guilt and so of pardon and reconciliation, is certainly a tremendous risk because she could end by losing sight of the gratuitous nature of salvation, the very *need* of salvation as the gift of the God who forgives sin. Salvation gets reduced to a problem of interpersonal relationships, the Gospel becomes a textbook for such relationships and people miss the very point for which Paul laboured so hard and which Jesus proclaimed in these words: "I did not come for good people but for sinners, not for the healthy but for the sick".

God freely justifies the sinner and this is the salvation which is continually offered to man. Man, who is incapable of a truly deep love, is made capable of love by the transforming power of the Spirit who purifies him. If we miss this essential point — the Spirit who freely purifies and makes men able to love, overcoming selfishness and the fear of death — we are no longer able to build up a Christian community, however hard we work at establishing good

49

relationships between people. There is certainly a great deal at stake as far as the sense of penitence and sin are concerned.

When it comes to giving advice about our personal experience of penance, people can be divided into two groups.

The first group finds that the old way of short, frequent confession is still viable. This way provides, as it were, milestones which help us to be purified of our daily sins and keep us aware of the free nature of salvation. For the person who finds this way easy, is used to it and can follow it without any problems, it is a grace; this means that the Lord is leading and will continue to lead him in this way.

However, there are some priests, and also men and women religious and layfolk who, having changed their rule of penance, have found it rather difficult to continue the practice of regular confession; they find it arduous, a bit formal, neither helpful nor stimulating. Having experienced this sort of difficulty myself, I looked for a way out of it. This simple and apparently paradoxical thought helped me: If I find short confession arduous, why not try to make it a bit longer? Here again is the reversal of a situation. So I came to an experience (shared by others, in groups or singly, in other parts of the world, too) of penitential dialogue; this has the effect of retaining the value of traditional confession but making it more personal.

What is meant by penitential dialogue? This means a dialogue with a representative of the Church, a priest in fact, in which I seek to experience reconciliation in a fuller way than is possible in a short confession where only one's faults are mentioned. The new penitential rite makes provision for just such an expansion of confession. It suggests, if possible, that it is best to start the dialogue by reading a Bible passage, a psalm for instance, selected for its appropriateness to the state of one's soul; then a prayer is said, perhaps extempore, which helps to create an atmosphere of reality. There follow three steps which I like to call: *confessio laudis, confessio vitae* and *confessio fidei.*

50

Confessio laudis: this is a repetition of Peter's experience in Luke 5. First of all, Peter realizes how great the Lord is, that Jesus has done a tremendous thing for him and has given him unexpected gifts. *Confessio laudis* means starting the penitential dialogue by answering the question: since my last confession, what should I chiefly thank God for? When has God been especially close to me, when have I felt his help and sensed his presence? To start by an expression of praise and thanksgiving, helps to put our life in the right perspective.

Then comes the *confessio vitae.* Of course I entirely agreed with the old practice of confessing one's sins in the light of the Ten Commandments or some such framework, but for the *confessio vitae* I would suggest — for those who can give the time to it — this question: Since my last confession, what is the thing I most regret before God? What weighs on my mind? Then, rather than trying to make a list of sins — the really serious ones will emerge spontaneously — we try to see the various events that weigh on our minds and which we wish had not happened. And precisely for this reason we bring them to God to be purified and delivered from them.

Here we see the true meaning of the *afesis amartion:* to take away a weight. This weight might be, for example, a dislike which we have been unable to overcome and although we cannot see clearly whether or not we have been at fault it has still weighed on our mind; or maybe we have been rather weary of well-doing, slow to love or to serve; these attitudes, because they are deeply-rooted, may have caused us to sin in other ways. In this way we take a good look at ourselves as we feel we really are. What would I have wished undone? What particularly weighs on my mind before God? From what specific thing do I wish God to free me? In this way it is easier to see ourselves as we are in our ever-changing circumstances, with our sins which are real enough but not always easy to describe; we may find that others are criticizing us while we cannot see ourselves clearly except by using this method.

Let us ask to be set free, because the power of God can

liberate us as people; let us not merely keep moral accounts with God! He wants to give us space, and new heart so that we can start again with new spontaneity.

Lastly comes the *confessio fidei* which is the immediate preparation for receiving God's forgiveness. This means saying to God: Lord, I know my weakness, but I know that you are stronger. I believe in your power in my life, I believe that you can save me just as I am. I entrust my sinfulness to you, risking everything, I put it into your hands and I am no longer afraid of it.

It is necessary, then, to experience salvation with trustfulness and joy, for this is the moment when God enters our lives and gives us the Good News: "Go in peace", I have taken upon myself the burden of your sins, your weariness, your lack of faith, your interior sufferings, your crosses. I have taken them all upon myself, I have taken the load so that you might be free.

That is but one of many methods: it seems to me that this sort of dialogue can be of real help to us; we shall want to repeat it of our own accord because it helps us to change for the better.

Confession is not just a duty: it is a joyful occasion to be sought after. Even in the ordinary confessions which so many people make, I sometimes feel it is good to ask those who confess in a hurry: is there not something in your life which you wish to thank God for? This question alone puts the dialogue on a different, less formal level and helps us to enter into the life of the person concerned.

We can and should help each other to come to the sort of penitence to which the Lord led Peter when he first called him. Let us ask the Lord to help us — as he helped Peter — to understand what he requires of us, what he promises us and is so ready to give us.

Jesus teaches his disciples

Faith and extra-faith ministries

We have already spoken of the charisms listed by Paul in Ephesians 4 : 11 — apostles, prophets, evangelists, pastors and teachers. Here is another passage which describes most kinds of ministry, the fruit of the Spirit (Romans 12 : 6-8): "For we have various gifts according to the grace given to each one of us. Let him who has the gift of prophecy use it according to the amount of faith he has, let ministers attend to their ministry, teachers to their teaching, those who exhort, to exhortation; let the man who gives do so with simplicity, let the man in authority act diligently, let the merciful man be cheerful". Or in 1 Corinthians 12 : 8-10, we read: "The same Spirit grants wise speech to one man, knowledge to another, faith to another, to another the gift of healing, and to another the power to work miracles, to prophesy, etc.". Again at the end of the chapter (1 Corinthians 12 : 28) there is a passage very like Ephesians 4 : 11 : "God has placed men in the Church first as apostles, secondly as prophets, thirdly as teachers . . . to others he has given the gifts of healing and helping, ruling, speaking other languages".

On the basis of these texts I would like to suggest a distinction which is useful in guiding us in the formation of evangelists.

1. There are some services in the Church which can be called 'extra-faith' ministries.

These are all the services which we render to our brothers as the outcome of our faith and baptism and conversion to Christ, but which can be done by many others and in collaboration with others: the care of the sick, handicapped and drug addicts, legal and social services, teaching, prisoners' aid. In any case, these are ministries, works of mercy and assistance of every kind which, for the Christian, arise from his faith but which, in themselves, can arise simply from a desire for humanity and solidarity with one's fellows. For the Christian, certainly, they have a particular quality because they are the fruit of mature faith but as far as their object is concerned they are indistinguishable from the services of non-Christians.

2. There are other services (above all the five recorded in Ephesians — apostles, prophets, evangelists, pastors and teachers) which are specifically faith ministries, which means that their object is the service of the faith.

The service of the faith includes the various forms of evangelization, the pastorate and the care and doctrinal instruction of the community. These two types of ministry are linked to one another: extra-faith ministries deal with human advancement, while faith ministries deal with evangelization, in which the faith itself is the gift given.

Certainly for the Christian a faith ministry is the greatest possible service he can render: if it is true that man has many different needs, his deepest need is surely for faith, hope and unlimited love.

All the other services to mankind are useful but the most glorious of all is the ministry of ministries, the one which gives man the strength to live and to hope. It is important to provide bread and justice and the chance to live a human life: but if one does not go on to give a man a profound reason for living, what is the use of giving him all the other things? The Christian serves mankind in a specifically Christian way knowing that such service is *indispensable* if all the other services are to lead to the satisfaction of all men's needs. This distinction will help us to understand Jesus' teaching in Luke (from chapter 5 to 18).

The education of the Christian

Exegetes are generally agreed that Luke 9:51 marks an important division in the text. At that moment Jesus begins his journey to Jerusalem. This division is peculiar to Luke: here the evangelist has condensed a whole series of words and sayings of Jesus. So the chapters can be divided clearly from 5 to 9 and from 9 to 18. If I had to give a title to these two parts, I would call them:

— the education of the Christian;
— the formation of the evangelist proper.

Obviously these two headings do not cover the entire scope of these chapters because the Gospel contains untold riches; when we choose a heading it is only to give a sample of the contents and to emphasize certain aspects while knowing that many more could be brought out.

Let us take a brief look at the contents of the first chapters, 5 to 9. Chapter 4 was the 'overture', the introduction of Jesus as the 'failed evangelist' and itself contains all Luke's basic themes, including suffering and death.

With chapter 5 begins the calling of the disciples, that is, the real start of Jesus' public activities. The contents of these chapters can be subdivided thus: first of all, there is a series of seven miracles. They are, so to speak, miracles in ascending order, because they culminate with the raising of a dead man. In brief, they are: the healing of the demoniac, Simon's mother-in-law, the leper, the paralytic, the man with the withered hand, the centurion's servant and the son of the widow of Nain. After a short pause there comes another series of miracles: the stilling of the storm, the Gadarene demoniac, the woman with a haemorrhage, the raising of Jairus' daughter, the multiplication of the loaves, the transfiguration, the healing of the epileptic.

There are fourteen miracles — two sets of seven — and then chapter 9 starts with: "Then he called the Twelve to him and gave them authority over all the devils and power to heal disease: and he sent them to proclaim the Kingdom of God and to heal the sick". It is interesting to note that power is given to the apostles after the first series of miracles.

Together with these miracles we have various sayings of Jesus: they may be roughly grouped under three headings: *teaching on fraternal duties* — love, mercy, the practical and courageous response to the demands made on us; *polemics* on the lack of faith and against the inhuman religious practices of the Pharisees (Luke 6:1-11);

Messianic teaching and the reversal of traditional values:
"Blessed are the poor . . . woe to you, rich men!" This is
the overall content of these chapters. This is the sort of
education received by Peter, James and John, the disciples
who follow Jesus, live with him and sit at his feet.

First of all Jesus seems to give them an *education as
Christians,* instilling in them those attitudes which make up
a mature man, able to recognise the needs and sufferings of
others. Think of the educational value of the miracles wit-
nessed by the disciples, miracles which embrace all sorts of
human suffering: from disease to disgrace, from obsessions
to physical and psychological pain.

The disciples who witness these things come in close
contact with these people and see how much evil there is
in the world, how much suffering, rejection and depravity,
and learn how to respond to each situation with love, sensitivity and empathy. They are given lessons in goodness,
charity and compassion for all the sufferings of men. They
are taught that openness of heart which was so characteristic
of Jesus; Peter, summing up Jesus' life, said: "He went
about doing good to all, healing all the oppressed" (Acts
10:38). Jesus teaches his disciples to share his own sensitive
and ready compassion and his capacity to see the suffering
and distress of others.

Secondly, the disciples learn about their relationship to
Jesus; they are taught to have faith in his mission as
Messiah. The apostles witness Jesus' goodness and success,
also his ability to conquer men's hearts; the apostles enthusiastically put their trust in him, with his uprightness and
straightforwardness, his sensitive awareness of the most
hidden sufferings of human hearts; their faith also grows in
the Master's ability as leader and guide.

Thirdly, Jesus teaches his disciples to look at men's
basic problems. Take for example Jesus' words to the
paralytic: "Your sins are forgiven"; or his statement: "I
did not come for the sake of the righteous but for sinners";
or his words about the woman in Simon's house: "Much

has been forgiven her, for she loved much". The disciples, like labouring men everywhere, probably had a very limited experience of life and their interests were probably confined to their own families and friends. Jesus teaches them that there is so much suffering, such a call for compassion, that people suffer interiorly and are bowed down with woe and in need of a consoling word.

That is what I mean by the education of Christians, Christian men, with the emphasis on the word 'men', that is, beings capable of turning in brotherliness to others. We must admit that this is the easiest way to preach Jesus because it is all so beautiful and obvious: brotherly love, compassion, charity; no man can find fault with that. Those parts of the Gospel are the best known the world over; Jesus can be appreciated as a great master of humanity even by the many young people, for example, who are not believers. Sometimes we see young people with no definite faith undertaking voluntary work; they willingly throw themselves into the task of helping and serving others; no one can say that this is a useless or strange choice on their part. So this first school of charity is important and the evangelist must pass through it. The priest in particular will be able to understand people's most hidden needs — the most subtle needs which are linked to the inmost personality — if he has some idea of the more immediate needs, such as sickness, hunger, loneliness and various kinds of alienation, and if he has developed a sensitivity to these things. Here the extra-faith ministries with their many forms of service and assistance to the poor are of supreme importance; these ministries are in fact essential stepping-stones to deeper things.

A truly mature Christian community is one which enables its baptized members to have plenty of this sort of experience and which trains its young people along these lines. Otherwise we run the risk of offering choice food to people without assessing their capacity to digest it; their actual needs may be more immediate and may have to be adapted to their circumstances.

We need to take this into account when training our

priests. It is good for priests to be trained in the sort of isolation which allows room for study, prayer, the discipline and austerity of life which are so necessary and without which men cannot stand up to the hardships of priestly life. However, it is equally fundamental for the priest to engage in, and never forget, the more practical side of Christian ministry. From time to time there are priests who, wishing to revitalize their own vocation, devote themselves for a while to the direct service of the poor and sick and thus discover the Gospel afresh, as well as recovering the sense of life as a gift. On the other hand, it can be said that our whole life through, we are bound to this sort of service; we should strive to understand the sick who are really the cream of society, we need to minister to those most in need of our help. For priests it is of course very important to help sick clergy; we can use this as a test to see whether or not we are being faithful to our education as Christians, for it is to the evangelical ministry, among thousands of possible ministries, that we have dedicated ourselves. We do well, too, to remember with gratitude the sick priests who pray fervently, offering their sufferings for the intentions of Pope and clergy alike.

We should indeed reflect the life of Christ in our charity towards our sick confreres; the official structures are not enough. We should, each of us, find time for sick visits, however many other things we have to do. Sick people are often subject to depression and fear, making them look on the black side of things; a visit can change all that and restore their peace and serenity. We never cease to learn these things and each of us is often prompted to ask: in my particular circumstances, how do I show forth the brother-liness and mercy which Christ taught his disciples, especially towards those afflicted by sickness and various other forms of poverty?

The formation of the evangelist

What are the characteristics of this second part? In this section, Jesus' miracles diminish in number. There are not more than five, some of which are very briefly recorded. After the blind man of Jericho (Luke 18:35-43), there are no more miracles. From the triumphal entry onwards, this part of Jesus' activity ceases completely. His sayings, on the other hand, are more frequent, especially the teaching given solely to the Twelve, the evangelists.

Thus it seems clear that during the second period of his life, Jesus devotes his time particularly to those who are close to him, in order to form them in a special way. Even Jesus' conversation with the people reflects this change. For example, chapter 12 begins: "Meanwhile, as thousands of people had come together and were treading on one another (in their anxiety to see Jesus), Jesus addressed himself *first of all to the disciples*". Verse 4 of the same chapter reads: "I say to you, my friends" and at verse 13 we have: "one of the crowd said to him" and Jesus answered him, but verse 22 has, "Then he said to his disciples". So it seems clear here that Jesus speaks a little to the people but is eager and willing to withdraw in order to speak to his own. He pays special attention to the Twelve.

What sort of sayings does Jesus use in this second period of his ministry? They are rather different from those in the first period, they are *the hardest and most intransigent sayings of the Gospel*, the ones which are hard to explain to members of the Church.

At one time, when only very short passages of the Gospel were read, they hardly ever appeared in the liturgy, whereas nowadays they do appear, and this leads to a difficulty. I myself experienced this difficulty one year when I had to expound these texts on television during the summer. "I have not come to bring peace but a sword, I have come to cause division, etc.". In a word, the sayings of the second part of St Luke are for those who have already come a certain way on their spiritual journey. So it is quite natural that someone quite new to the Gospel may be offended and retain a wrong and incorrect impression.

Let us now look at the three most prominent themes in these sayings of Jesus.

First of all, there is *training in detachment and liberty*

of heart. "Sell what you have and give it to the poor; make yourselves purses which will not wear out, and an inexhaustible treasure in heaven where thieves do not steal and moths do not consume it, for your treasure will be in the same place as your heart; be ready with your belt fastened and your lamps lit. . .". The man who lives close to Jesus gradually acquires liberty of heart, learning not to be attached to any of the things which could distract him from his task: wages, self-interest, a career, personal preoccupations. Jesus stresses the necessity of a free heart and detachment, in the strongest of terms.

Secondly there is *learning abandonment of oneself to the Father.* The disciple must know that, having decided to follow Jesus, his life is in the Father's hands and he should trust in him. He must entrust his present and future life to him. "What father will give his son a stone if he asks for bread? . . . so if you, who are evil, know how to give good things, how much more will your heavenly Father give the good Spirit to those who ask him" (Luke 11:11-13).

Or again: "So I tell you: don't keep thinking about your life, and about what you will have to eat; nor about your body and what you will wear. Life is worth more than food and the body more than clothes. Look at the ravens: they neither sow nor reap nor store food in barns and God feeds them. You are worth so much more than birds! Which of you, however hard you try, can add even an hour to his span of life? So if you cannot do even the smallest thing, why worry about the rest? See how the lilies grow: they neither spin nor weave and yet I tell you that even Solomon in all his glory was not clothed as beautifully as one of them. If God clothes the grass of the fields like that, which flowers today and tomorrow is thrown on the fire, how much more will he clothe you, you who are so lacking in faith? So don't go looking for food and drink and don't be anxious: worldly men worry over such things; but your Father knows that you need them. Rather, seek the Kingdom of God and all these things will be given you as well. Don't be afraid, little flock, for your Father is pleased to give you the Kingdom" (Luke 12:22-32).

As we have already seen it is of prime importance for men to trust. Here, the trust has a specific object: it is the Father who knows even the number of hairs on our heads. The Father will not abandon you, you should trust him. Jesus asks this of those whom he prepares to be evangelists.

The third and last theme which recurs at intervals is this: *teaching about the meaning of the Cross*. This is not mentioned in the first chapters but only comes out at a certain point where *three* predictions of the Passion appear between chapters 9 and 18. The first is chapter 9:22: "The Son of Man must suffer greatly, be rejected by the elders, chief priests and scribes, and be put to death and he will rise again on the third day. The second prediction is in chapter 9:44 and the third in chapter 18:3. The three predictions provide a frame for the nine chapters and give some idea of their overall meaning: Jesus is teaching his disciples to have a sense of the Cross.

A living education

All evangelical training should have this very important characteristic: it should be on a practical rather than merely ideological plane. Jesus states principles and draws conclusions or he sets forth a programme and then expounds the successive points in practice. It is a living education: the disciples live with Jesus, they see how he reacts in a given situation, how he speaks and behaves. So teaching and life are intertwined. Jesus both acts and teaches: this is fundamental to evangelical training. The Gospel makes an impression because of the way it is lived by the Lord and his disciples. That is why, when we talk of a 'school of discipleship' in the Church's tradition it is always a living relationship of master and disciple. This is how people learn things. If we look back on our own experience, we can say that what we have learned came to us above all through contact with true Christians; the grace of good and devout parents, meeting some priest who made a particular impression on us; their words, actions, reactions and silences, their comments at appropriate times, all these taught us a great deal. In the same way, others learn from us: it is not so much what we say but our way of living, reacting and judging which influences others. Jesus himself wished this and it is he who started this type of practical school; all the different kinds of pastoral initiation which brings the evangelist in contact with the people, are extremely useful whenever there is this sort of 'osmosis' or invisible transmission of values.

Some time ago I read a study on the ways of communicating the meaning of life, in which the author listed a series of media: inter-suggestivity, symbols, language and example. From this list it is obvious that *language* is only one of the means whereby values are communicated and often not the most adequate means. There is such a thing as inter-suggestivity, which occurs simply by people being together, without anything actually being said. For example, a bishop and his clergy in retreat are saying something inexpressible in words: simply by being together, seeking to listen and pray, they are affirming their common faith and ministry, they are listening to the same Word; they are also saying something about the relationship of the bishop to his clergy and their desire to go forward together. All this is communicated simply by being together and there is no need to express it in words. All sorts of life values are similarly communicated. For example, a mother holding a child in her arms assumes a profound and rich significance which speaks volumes. Then we have *symbols:* symbols, gestures, all forms of art and song, say much more than words can express. However, language is necessary, otherwise certain symbols lack clarity and will remain ambiguous.

Above all, there is *incarnate life*, personalities who incarnate values: it is these which play an important role in the transmission of values. If these personalities are linked in communal inter-suggestivity, and use well-chosen symbols, their influence will be still greater.

Consider the parables of Jesus, his gestures, the Cross as the fundamental symbol of his love, inexhaustible in meaning. We begin to see how Jesus formed his disciples; he taught them in such a way that they were unable at first to understand the meaning of what he said and did.

Let us ask ourselves at this point: *what is the result of this careful, well-balanced education given by Jesus according to all the rules?* It is disappointing and the Gospel itself says so. The Gospel does not hide from us the fact that all this marvellous use of educational devices was of very little use in forming evangelists.

These words appear at the beginning of these nine chapters in which the evangelist is being formed in the ministry of faith, in attitudes of detachment, abandonment to the Father and understanding of the Cross, all of which are necessary in order freely to proclaim the Gospel: "While everyone was astonished at the things he was doing, he said to his disciples: Get this into your heads: the Son of Man will be delivered into the hands of men. — But they did not understand what he said to them; it puzzled them so much that they could make no sense of it and they were afraid to ask him what it meant" (Luke 9:43).

So the Evangelist insists, rather bitterly, on this lack of comprehension: they did not understand, it was a mystery to them, they could make no sense of it and they were afraid to ask. It was the sort of mental block which occurs when things go round in one's head but are so foreign to one's way of thinking that one dares not break the spell, and so fears remain unsubdued.

It is a paradoxical situation: *Jesus speaks, clearly predicting the path he is to tread and his disciples follow him without understanding and are afraid to question him.* This is in fact a real misunderstanding between Jesus and his disciples: they are agreed on so many points, but this one point, so fundamental to Jesus, they resolutely refuse to accept. Luke is bold enough to reintroduce this theme — nine chapters later — at the end of this period of training, just before the entry into Jerusalem and the last miracle, the healing of the blind man of Jericho: "Then he took the Twelve on one side and said to them: See, we are going to Jerusalem and all that the prophets wrote concerning the Son of Man will be fulfilled. He will be handed over to the pagans, mocked, shamed, spat on, and after flogging him they will kill him and on the third day he will rise again. And they understood none of this, they found his words obscure and they did not understand what he had said" (Luke 18:31-34). Three times this fact is stressed: nine chapters of life together with Jesus have made no impression at all as far as this point is concerned. This is of interest to us because it shows us that the training of an evangelist is a difficult task, it comes up against a certain secret resistance. Until we have really understood and penetrated their meaning, the words go over our heads; or perhaps they even enter our minds, we echo them on our lips, but *they have not reached our hearts*. When the Gospel is preached to the disciples of Emmaus, before meeting Jesus, we can see how the words had entered their minds but had gone out again without making their hearts 'burn'; this is the reason for the suffering, anguish and difficulty of the evangelist.

In the next section of Luke's Gospel, let us ask ourselves: why was there such difficulty — surely it is unheard of? — what happened to the disciples' souls to prevent their understanding the mystery of Christ? The answer to this fundamental question will throw light on so many crises in our own evangelistic work, so many moments of disappointment, discouragement, obstruction and lack of co-operation. God will help us to resolve this question, not by force of argument or teeth-gritting determination but by the releasing power of the Spirit in our hearts. It is the power of the Spirit which we should invoke as the joyful and glorious power of salvation.

The way of Peter, the first evangelist

Peter, better than anyone else, shows us the path Jesus makes his disciples tread in order to become evangelists. So let us consider Peter's experience in following Jesus.

Twice Peter confesses himself a sinner. Luke 5:8: "Seeing this, Simon Peter threw himself on his knees before Jesus saying: Leave me, Lord, for I am a sinner", and Luke 22:62 reads: "And going out, Peter wept bitterly". What we need to ask is: what is the difference between the first and second occasions; what is the spiritual journey Peter has travelled between one and the other and how is the truth of the second occasion much deeper than that of the first?

On the first occasion, Peter is called "fisher of men" but, as we shall see, he was still fairly incapable of understanding the mystery of the Gospel. On the second occasion, Peter reaches, so to speak, the high point of his preparation as an evangelist. Let us look at the journey taken by Peter between his call and his denial. How did Peter reach this point, what stages did he pass through? His experience is important for the whole Church as Jesus affirms: "Satan wanted to sift you like wheat, but I have prayed for you that your faith may not fail and when you have repented, you must strengthen your brothers" (Luke 22:31-32). So Peter's experience, once again, can be useful to us, to strengthen us. Next let us consider why Peter denied Jesus, how he so misunderstood the kerygma that he did worse than the people of Nazareth and rejected Jesus from his life; finally, in what way did this denial subsequently enable Peter to preach the Gospel?

Peter's confession and failure to understand

Luke gives us Peter's confession but not his repudiation, when he tries to prevent Jesus from choosing his own path. Mark records both. In Mark 8:29 Jesus asks: "Whom do

you say that I am? Peter answered: You are the Christ".
This is the supreme moment of Peter's mission; he truly
becomes an evangelist, prophet and apostle able to sum up
other people's thoughts and give them a precise expression.
At that moment, Peter is filled with joy, he has justified the
faith Jesus had placed in him. This is why he is dismayed
to hear Jesus saying: "The Son of Man must suffer greatly
and be rejected by the elders and chief priests and scribes;
then he will be killed and the third day he will rise again.
Jesus spoke openly of this. Then Peter took him aside and
started to rebuke him. But he turned and, looking at the
disciples, rebuked Peter and said to him: Get away from
me, Satan! You don't think as God thinks but as men do"
(Mark 8: 31-33).

What impression did these words make on Peter and
how did they affect his mood? Peter must have thought:
but what have I done wrong to make him treat me like
this? After all, I wanted the best for him, I wanted to prevent his coming to such a sad end, I wanted him to be
honoured as he deserves; truly I do not understand this
Master of mine, nothing is going well for him, he has
ideas which are quite beyond me, he is angry with me and
won't look at me anymore. Peter is going through a difficult
time; he feels that he understands Jesus but not completely.

This misunderstanding is soon swallowed up by a fresh
event which fills Peter with joy again: "About eight days
after this conversation, Jesus took Peter, John and James
with him and climbed a mountain to pray" (Luke 9: 28). In
the episode of the transfiguration, we can see how enthusiastically and responsibly Peter fulfills his calling: "He said
to Jesus: Master, it is good for us to be here; let us make
three tents, one for you, one for Moses and one for Elijah;
he did not know what he was saying" (Luke 9: 33).

Here Peter shows his great generosity. He does not say:
Let's make a tent for me, too. Peter thinks of Jesus, Moses
and Elijah; he is the man who, feeling himself included in
the Kingdom of God, takes all the responsibility for it; he
is quick to take action, to make decisions and provide for
the Kingdom himself. At that moment, he feels at the height

of his powers and abilities and when he goes down the mountain on the following day (Luke 9:37) and sees the other apostles unable to cast a devil out of a boy, we can well imagine him echoing Jesus' words: "What a perverse and unbelieving people you are! How long do I have to stay with you and put up with you?" (Luke 9:41). Peter thinks: I have really got faith, I am on his side, these other apostles have not got the message yet, when it comes to understanding the power of Jesus, they simply aren't up to my high standard. Peter is in fact becoming increasingly aware of the burden of responsibility laid on his shoulders.

And now there comes another shower of cold water for Peter. After many other events (let us pass over the intervening ones and come to those immediately preceding the Passion), Jesus addresses him: "Simon, Simon, Satan wanted to sift you like wheat, but I have prayed that your faith may not fail and when you have repented, you must strengthen your brothers. And Peter said to him: Lord, I am ready to go to prison and to death with you. He answered: Peter, I tell you: before the cock crows you will have denied knowing me three times" (Luke 22:31-34).

How did Peter take these words, certainly of great importance to him: "strengthen your brothers"?

At first they make him think that obviously he has a good understanding of Christ's message, he has mastered it and understands it thoroughly: "Lord, I am ready to go to prison and death with you". When we hear these words read, we say that they are full of presumption, but we say that in the light of the subsequent events; but in themselves they are very fine words, words which every Christian should be able to repeat. Even if we examine them from a psychological point of view, what can we find negative about them which could give us any hint of Peter's forthcoming fall? Peter is truly expressing what he feels but it is quite clear that he had paid no heed to Jesus' words: "Satan wanted to sift you like wheat, but I have prayed for you".

If he had been listening, he would have said: "Lord, thank you for praying for me; I know how weak I am, I can

67

do so little, stay near me". Instead (and here we meet the same problem which we saw first in Nazareth), Peter regards the Gospel, the task he has been given, as a privilege, something he owns and may dispose of in his own strength, and not a gift which must be constantly and humbly asked of the Lord. Just as the people of Nazareth would have liked to use Jesus' power for their own ends and rebel when the Master shows them that God's power has no limits and that Nazareth is not necessarily the only place appointed for the mystery of salvation, so Peter gradually appropriates the task of evangelization: it is his, it belongs to him, it gives him certain privileges, a certain strength and courage and precisely because it is his, he is ready to take the consequences on himself.

All unwittingly, he is riding for a fall. *In fact the Gospel is God's free gift, it is the salvation which God freely grants to the sinner and as long as we accept it with thankful hearts, with gratitude and humility, we have the right attitude;* but as soon as we start to appropriate it, to treat it as our property, we completely reverse the situation. Then *we* become masters of the Gospel and the Church, masters of the situation and we are no longer people who receive the gift and pass it on but people who have taken it over for themselves.

It is by degrees that Peter falls into this error: he was already on the wrong path when he wanted to pitch tents for everyone on the mountain, when it seemed to him that he should take the situation in hand in his role as chief steward of the Kingdom, thinking himself able to handle the mysteries of God. For this reason, he has to have the lesson of falling into the most humiliating weakness as man and evangelist — the inability to face up to an awkward situation.

To return to the text, which is psychologically most revealing, Jesus "then said: When I sent you out without purse, knapsack or sandals, did you lack anything? They answered: Nothing. Then he added: but now, let him who has no sword sell his coat and buy one. For I tell you: these words of Scripture must be fulfilled by me: He was counted among the criminals. In fact, everything written of me is about to take place. They said: Lord, here are two swords. But he replied: That is enough!" (Luke 22:35-38). Certainly behind the Twelve, once again, is Peter, always eager to save the situation; having failed to understand Jesus' words, he says: I will defend you with the sword, leave it to me, you can rely on me, I'll make sure your enemies don't get the better of you.

Peter is not cowardly and fearful, he does not act like this because he himself is afraid of the cross, he is utterly sincere. His mistake lies in wanting to play the main part himself. Putting it theologically, we could say that he wants to save Jesus, he wants to be the saviour of the Lord.

The crisis for Peter

At this point we come to the episode of the Garden of Olives: Jesus, in agony, sweats blood and is left without any of the disciples to keep him company, not even Peter. Peter cannot stand the sight of Jesus' weakness and his image of the Master starts to disintegrate: he knew him as the powerful and victorious Lord, always successful, with a word to meet every situation, the man whose swift reasoning could defeat the most captious enemy.

Now for the first time, Peter sees Jesus overcome by weakness and he feels a tremendous uneasiness in his heart: how is it possible for God to be with this man if this man is afraid and shows himself to be so frail?

Peter had learned from the Old Testament to see God as great and powerful; Yahweh who conquers in battle and defeats his enemies. In his mind, Peter had transferred all this power to Jesus but now that he sees this weakness, what else can he do but close his eyes and not think about it? It is the gesture of someone who says: I dont' want to know, I cannot understand. The weakness shown by Jesus causes Peter to collapse interiorly, because it is quite the opposite of his idea of the Kingdom of God; he had envisaged a Kingdom which would always be victorious and that is why he said, when Jesus first foretold his Passion: No, Lord, this must not happen to you, it will never happen because the power of Yahweh is within you. Now he doubts whether God is with this man, he thinks God is deserting Jesus, and he is devastated.

Then comes Jesus' arrest. Judas, the guards, the kiss of betrayal. What does Peter do at that moment? He summons all his strength: "Lord, shall we strike them with the sword? And one of them — (Luke does not name him, but the other evangelists do) — struck the high priest's servant and cut off his right ear" (Luke 22:49-50).

Peter is once more the hero who wants to die for the Master, he wants to throw himself into the fray, win at all costs, perhaps die, to save him. Peter feels that the supreme price is being asked of him: the Gospel demands this of me, I am called to give my life, so I must give it.

Imagine his complete dismay and inner anguish when Jesus intervenes: "Leave them alone, that's enough! And touching the ear, he heals it. Then Jesus said to those who had come to meet him, the high priests, captains of the Temple guard and elders: have you come out with swords and sticks as if I were an outlaw? I have been with you daily in the Temple and you never laid a hand on me; but this is your hour when darkness reigns" (Luke 22:51-53). So Jesus himself allows the power of darkness to run its course. Peter realizes that all his plans have gone wrong; he wanted to fight with the Master for the Kingdom of Light and the Master stands there, unarmed, accepting the sway of the Kingdom of Darkness. His whole idea of God is shattered. God is no longer a god of power, goodness and justice, he does not intervene to save Jesus. Who, then, is this Master in whom we have believed?

Peter is plunged into a tremendous inner confusion which makes it easy for us to understand all his denials; if we look at it like this, as Luke's Gospel presents it to us, we see how subtly the Evangelist throws light on Peter's psychology: he no longer knows what he wants himself.

Peter follows the Master but from a distance. He follows him because he loves him; from a distance, because he can no longer openly take his side, because he does not understand him. What, in fact does he want? If he wants us to act bravely, we are ready, if he wants something else, he should say so and at least make it clear to us!

And here is the first question: "This one was with him too. But he denied it saying: Woman, I do not know him". Note the subtlety, which may or may not be intentional, of this phrase: "with him". It is the very phrase which Peter had used a short time before: "Lord I am ready to go with you to prison and death". Now he can no longer respond to this "with him" and says: "I don't know him". In fact the negation "I don't know him" has a certain truth in it for Peter because Jesus is no longer the man Peter thought he was, that is, a leader, a chief, a victor, a man who can triumph over adverse circumstances. He no longer knows or understands this man who is given over to the power of his enemies, he no longer knows what he wants, this Jesus who is so different from Peter's previous image of him. It is quite true that Peter no longer knows him.

When he is confronted a second time: "You are one of them too!", Peter denies again, "No, I am not!" I feel there is a touch of contempt in this answer: they ran away, I at least wanted to do something for him, I wanted to give my life and I would have given it if he had let me. I am neither one of those who gave way to craven fear, nor am I with him because I no longer recognize him. The text says: "About an hour went by". We can imagine Peter's identity crisis during that hour: who am I, what do I want, what has my life been all about, why did I decide to follow this man, who made me do it? Yet I believed in him, I wish him well, he should not have let me down like this. All the inner turmoil of a man who has generously followed a path and at a certain moment, no longer understands God's will for him.

What does God want of me now? Before, I could have said what it was, until a few hours ago I was ready to die with him and now I no longer know what God wants. It is undoubtedly a terrible hour for Peter. And when it had gone by, "someone else insisted: Surely this man was with him too; he is also a Galilean. But Peter said: I don't know what you're saying, man".

I don't know if the Evangelist uses this phrase intentionally or not: "I don't know what you're saying" is the same as in the account of the transfiguration: "he did not know what he was saying". On the mountain, Peter thought he held the keys of the Kingdom by right of ownership and now he is reduced to saying, "I don't know what you are saying" when he has been asked a perfectly straightforward question on his geographical and cultural identity: are you a Galilean or not?

The trial Jesus allows Peter to go through is one of the most terrible that can face a man, when he starts to doubt his whole religious training and formation: is this the God in whom I have believed? Is this really the will of God for me or have I made a dreadful mistake?

If Peter has gone through this, he has gone through it on behalf of the whole Church, for all of us; he has gone through it in order to strengthen the brethren; so it is a trial which he has undergone as head of the Church and chief of evangelists. For it is not possible to be an evangelist unless we allow ourselves to be so upset by God's plan that we come to realize that it is *his* plan and not ours, his Gospel and not ours, his salvation, not ours.

Peter's dilemma can in fact be simply expressed like this: Peter wanted to save Jesus, but in fact it was Jesus who had to save Peter and Peter had to realize that he was saved and pardoned by Jesus; he was in fact the first depositary of the pardon and mercy of the Gospel. This cost him a tremendous amount because he was very proud of his faithfulness and capacity to be loyal and upright. Instead the Lord shows him that he, too, can become totally bewildered and so, if he wants to preach the Gospel, he must first of all have an unlimited understanding of the saving mercy of God and unlimited compassion for his brothers in the Church. The text continues: "At that moment, while he was still speaking, a cock crowed". The crowing of the cock is the denunciation of his sin: this is what you have come to, you who thought to possess the Kingdom and the Gospel, to be the defender of the Master.

This biting denunciation, cold and accusing, would indeed be terrible if the Lord had not suddenly looked at him: "Then the Lord turned and looked at Peter and Peter remembered the words which the Lord had said to him: Before the cock crows today, you will deny me three times. And going out he wept bitterly".

The experience of letting oneself be loved

Let us try to understand the difference between this incident and the other occasion on which Peter had said: "Leave me, Lord, I am a sinner". The words are substantially the same but how different is the experience! In the boat, Peter had been somewhat surprised when confronted with the power of God who had given him that huge catch of fish; he was aware of the difference between God's power and his own poverty but he was not really aware of his need of God's mercy. He could become, eventually, a dispenser of God's pardon, a person who could follow Jesus and serve others; he did not realize that he himself was the prime object of that mercy, the first to need the word of salvation.

Here, on the other hand, the Lord brings Peter as it were inexorably, to the point where he sees who he really is and his grief can be simply expressed thus: Lord I am a poor wretch like everyone else, Lord I never thought I'd come to this, Lord have mercy on me, Lord you are going to die for me when I have been unfaithful to you.

At this point Peter finally grasps what the Gospel is in terms of salvation for sinful man, he grasps the true nature of God. For God is not someone who urges us to do better, not a moral reformer of humanity but above all he is unlimited, boundless Love, offered freely and purely with a mercy which neither condemns nor accuses nor reproves. Jesus' look is not accusing or admonitory, it is simply a look of mercy and love: Peter, I love you even like this, I knew you were like this and I loved you knowing you were like this.

In conclusion we can say: Peter undergoes the *experience*, which is perhaps the easiest and the hardest in life, *of letting himself be loved*. Up until now he had always

73

prided himself on being the first to do things and now he understands that with God he can do nothing but let himself be loved, let himself be saved, let himself be pardoned. John's Gospel is saying more or less the same thing in the episode of the foot-washing: "You will not wash my feet; I'll wash yours". How hard it is to be beholden to someone!

The Gospel means, in fact, thanking God for absolutely everything, knowing that we are firmly upheld by his mercy and saving power.

It is at his own expense that Peter gains this intuition which will enable him later to be the first evangelist, the strengthener of the brethren, the first to proclaim the Word. He wanted to die for Jesus but now he sees that in fact it is Jesus who wants to die for him and the cross from which he wanted to save the Lord is the sign of love, salvation and availability of God for him.

Here we see that reversal of religious ideas which is just as difficult for every one of us; for at heart, we believe God is asking something of us, that he is bent on crushing or scolding us and we cannot grasp the evangelical picture of the God who serves, who puts his life at our disposal, as we can see every day in the Eucharist. "I am among you as one who serves"; "This is my Body, given for you"; before asking anything of you, I simply ask you to let me love you utterly.

So Peter comes to a genuine experience of the Gospel, as he grasps the fact that God's strong love completely encompasses the life of man. Let us ask God to show us, as he showed Peter, the extent of his mercy which is expressed in so many and diverse ways in men's lives.

It has been rightly said that, in her autobiography, St Thérèse of the Child Jesus had a perfect grasp of this evangelical spirit; even without any experience of sin and betrayal, she understood perfectly the substance of the Gospel: God loves us, he goes before us, he surrounds us with a boundless love, and therefore man can rest secure and can enter bravely on the path of faith, whence all Christian experience is born. Here we are at the very heart of the understanding of redeemed man in his encounter with the word of salvation which reveals him to himself. Let us pray for understanding that we may preach this Good News of salvation with our lips and with our lives.

Jesus the evangelist in the Passion

"What was once gain for me, I now consider loss on account of Christ. In fact, I now value nothing in comparison with the sublime knowledge of Christ Jesus my Lord, for whom I have left all these things, as so much rubbish, so that I may win Christ and be found in him, not with my own righteousness derived from the Law, but with the righteousness which comes from faith in Christ, God's righteousness, based on faith" (Philippians 3 : 7-9).

This is the point which Peter has reached when Jesus looks at him. He knows that he can no longer rely on his own capacity to follow the Master; it is through faith in Christ as Saviour that he is saved and able to follow him.

The text continues: "That I might know him and the power of his resurrection, by sharing his sufferings and being like him in death with the hope of attaining to the resurrection of the dead" (vv. 10-11). Starting from this passage, we can pray thus:

Thank you, Lord, because by showing Peter his weakness, you revealed to him your goodness and mercy and offered him your own strength.

Thank you, Lord, that you show your strength to us, too. Help us to share intimately in your sufferings, so that we come to a deep knowledge of your power as evangelist and saviour, so that we may share in the power of your resurrection.

Lord, we are always trying to escape from this path, we would like to share the power of your resurrection at once, without sharing your death; teach us, instead, as you taught Peter, to become partakers of your sufferings.

Help us to pass aright through the experience of the cross; may we receive it as the Gospel, the Good News, the power of God for our salvation, as something which restores us, helps us to understand the meaning of life, giving us realism, truth and courage; not as something which oppresses, crushes and frightens us.

Mother of God, you who followed Jesus in his Passion and sorrowfully shared in all his trials, teach us to share his sufferings in truth and simplicity and openness of heart so that we may join with you in the joy of the Risen Lord.

Grant this, O Father, You who sent Jesus to die and rise again for us, and now give us the fullness of the Spirit, for the glory of Christ who is alive here in our midst and in the whole Church throughout the world and in the hearts of men everywhere. Now and forever. Amen.

From the moment when Jesus looked at him, Peter suddenly realized the truth about himself and about Jesus; he knew what his attitude should be to the mystery of salvation.

However, Jesus has to go on teaching Peter the meaning of the Gospel, as he does all of us. It is in his Passion that he reveals himself as the great Evangelist sent from the Father. It is not for nothing that St John, referring to the Passion, says: "We have seen the glory of God" (John 1:14).

At one time, people used to meditate more often on the Passion — (witness the once widespread devotion of the Way of the Cross); people were able to reflect on the Lord's sufferings and his many sorrows; the accent was on Jesus suffering through the world's injustice and the system which crushed him, which symbolized the unjust conditions under which many poor folk lived.

Today, we tend to place the emphasis on Jesus' role in the Passion as Saviour and Redeemer. It comes naturally to us to pray like this: Thank you, Lord, for loving me as much as that, thank you for what you have done for me.

We should indeed reflect on what Jesus the Saviour and Redeemer has done for us, not in order to accuse ourselves of sloth but in order to encourage ourselves, to open our hearts afresh to the Master who loves, understands and is close to us.

In fact, our meditation on the Passion is coloured by our various experiences of life: the more we experience difficulties, our own or others' — humiliations, loneliness, serious illness, straitened circumstances — the more profoundly will we understand that, truly, God's revelation in the suffering Christ is one of the keys to human existence. Without this understanding, there are countless situations in which we really would not know what to say either to ourselves or to others.

To get a clear picture of Jesus our Redeemer, the Evangelist sent from the Father, we should read chapters 22 and 23 of Luke. It is true that the four evangelists give very similar accounts of the Passion: in fact, as this is the most ancient and most traditional narrative, it is likely to have fewer variations. Nevertheless, Luke, while following the traditional framework, makes several typical omissions as well as characteristic emphases, both of which serve to give a picture of Jesus as faithful Witness, Master and Evangelist.

For example, these incidents are peculiar to Luke: Jesus' look at Peter, the exhortation to the women and to the city of Jerusalem, the pardon of those who crucified him, and the reconciliation of the penitent thief. These are all incidents which show Jesus as the Evangelist *par excellence* precisely at the most dramatic moment of his life.

Let us now look at three passages from the Passion narrative. The first is that of *Jesus humiliated* and refers above all to the insults Jesus receives in the judgment hall, during his hearing before the tribunal. The second is *Jesus tempted*. Lastly, the most beautiful scene of the whole Passion is that where Jesus receives the penitent thief; *Jesus the Evangelist* can be most fully seen in this encounter. This is the culmination of Jesus' mission as he brings God's salvation to a wretched, lost man.

Jesus humiliated

The humiliations of Jesus: "Meanwhile the men who stood guard over Jesus mocked him, hit him and blindfolded him saying: Guess who hit you. And they insulted him in many other ways" (Luke 22 : 63-65). The persecution of Christian and non-Christian alike has made this scene tremendously relevant; we have only to read, always with deep humility, some of the accounts of those who have experienced these things for themselves.

Let us pause for a moment and try to understand how Jesus experienced this sort of persecution.

Peter gives an interpretation of what happened to Jesus in his first letter: "He did not commit any sin, nor was he guilty of deception. When insulted he did not insult in return and when he suffered he did not threaten revenge but committed his case to the One who judges justly" (1 Peter 2 : 22-23).

Of course this passage is based on Isaiah 53, the Song of the Suffering Servant, which is read again in this context: a man who is silent in the face of those who torture and kill him.

What is the human significance of this scene? Who and what offends Jesus in this way? They are guards, servants, that is, people who in their turn are used to being humiliated and offended by their superiors, used to the fact that the strongest man wins and one has to 'take it' from him. Usually they are the ones to be humiliated, despised, ordered to do the most laborious and useless fatigue duty without being able to rebel. But this time they find someone weaker and more vulnerable than themselves. See how the misery of the human condition comes out, when men unleash their baser instincts on one another; these men have so often been oppressed and beaten, perhaps for no good reason, and now they can vent their anger on someone weaker than themselves. Their life is bitter and burdensome with no outlet, none of the joys of family life; they are simply giving expression to what they are. It is not wickedness or pure spite: it is really the suffering of men in an intolerable situation who let out their feelings on Jesus.

What do they do to Jesus? Certainly they provoke him and attack what is dearest to him, his role as a prophet, he who is the "Word of the Father". "Guess who hit you!" They insult him as a man who can read human hearts and who can proclaim the truth. And what are they thinking as they do this? Perhaps they are wondering fearfully: why doesn't this man react, what is it that stops him from shielding himself from us? He is not the prophet we thought he was. Perhaps they are even disappointed because they were expecting a violent reaction and are confused and upset by all this.

How does Jesus react? Whilst Luke gives us to understand that Jesus responds with silence, John says that Jesus is silent for a while and then quietly asks his tormentors for an explanation: "If I have done you any wrong, tell me; if not, why do you hit me?" (John 18:23).

Here we have Jesus the Evangelist who, at the very moment when he is being so badly treated, makes a profound appeal to the humanity of the man who is hitting him, trying to reason with him: why are you doing this? Because you are unhappy inside, you are interiorly humiliated and oppressed; try to understand your own deepest desires. Hit me, if you like, but discover what your own desires really are, what you really want to be as a man. Jesus says this in words and even more by his silence. Certainly he excuses these men in his heart, he understands their roughness and brutality; he understands that very little of what they do is their own fault, and he offers himself for them. He offers himself for their salvation as the meek Word of the Father.

We find it very difficult to understand why God should have revealed himself in such weakness, why Jesus should have allowed this wickedness to take its course, thinking to heal it with patience rather than with punishment and reproof.

Let us ask God to help us truly to understand this mystery of God's weakness revealed in Jesus, the weakness of a defenceless and persecuted Church from which in fact an incredibly glorious Church is born. We can see it around us, too; we can see that from countries such as Poland come wonderful examples of Christian vitality, faith and commitment; it is a Church which certainly also defended itself courageously by word and by active resistance, but it has always been partially defenceless and weak, never resorting to arms and violence, always calm and constant in faith, un-ashamed of Christ's cross and humiliation.

Only a more extensive consideration of salvation history would bring home to us the truth that out of weakness immense strength is born; this very weakness bears witness to unarmed and defenceless humanity, crying out its resistance to injustice.

The Word of God shows us that the Lord's power is manifested not only in action but also in suffering, suffering with the sort of humility, simplicity and gentleness which is profoundly dignified. Looking at this scene, we may ask who is in fact the victor, who represents man's true dignity? Certainly it is Jesus who represents the true, righteous man at his most profound, the man who by his gentleness can overcome those who hurl themselves against him; he confuses and frightens them with his unusual behaviour.

Jesus tempted

The temptations of Jesus on the Cross: "The people stood by to watch but their leaders mocked him saying: He saved others, let him save himself if he is the Christ, God's Chosen One. The soldiers mocked him also and came up to offer him vinegar and said: If you are the King of the Jews, save yourself. There was also an inscription over his head: 'This is the King of the Jews'. One of the criminals hanging on the cross insulted him: You're the Christ, aren't you? Save yourself and us" (Luke 23 : 35-39).

There seems to me to be a similarity here with the first temptations of Jesus in the desert. "If you are the Son of God, tell these stones to change to bread; if you are the Son of God, throw yourself down". Here Jesus is being tempted to use his messianic power for his own ends; behind such a temptation lies the idea, developed in the whole of the Old Testament, of the power of God: "If you are the Christ of God, save yourself, if you are the King of the Jews, come down". That is to say: if he really represents our mental image of God the powerful ruler, let him prove it.

This is a dramatic moment for Jesus. If he listened to

F

these people and came down from the cross, everyone would believe in him. But if he comes down from the cross, how will he reveal a God who accepts death out of love for mankind? He will certainly reveal a powerful and successful God, a God whom one could use to further one's own ambitions, but he will no longer reveal the God who is not to be found anywhere in the history of religion — man on his own can never imagine such a deity — a God who serves, gives his life for man, who loves man enough to strip himself of everything for love of him, even to the point of self-annihilation.

It is this very idea of a domineering, demanding, impatient God, seeking men for his own ends, which Jesus came to destroy. The Gospel reveals a God of mercy who empties himself for love of mankind. A God of this sort always seems slightly incredible to us; we feel a bit diffident because it is difficult for man to accept; as it was hard for Peter to accept that his Master should die for him or should wash his feet. Yet it is this revolutionary, incredible image of God which Jesus reveals in all its depth, in his body, in his own flesh on the Cross; and the others try to dissuade him from this: save yourself, use your power, show that you can be master of the situation. Instead, Jesus came to show us how to serve.

We can never look at this scene enough. Here we are at the very heart of the Gospel and, by the grace of God, we have a constant means of reverting to it, for this is the Eucharist, Christ nourishing us in the form of bread: This is my Body, this is my Blood, given for you. Do this in remembrance of me.

Naturally this changes one's whole outlook on life: we too should be people who can be stripped, who can forget ourselves for the sake of others. Perhaps we always baulk slightly at this concept of God precisely because if we accepted it we would have to change our own attitude to life.

When we contemplate Christ crucified, we come to see the Church not as a body which serves its own ends but which ministers to all man's needs, especially his deepest needs: truth, love, justice, faith and hope. As we contemplate Christ crucified we come to see that for a man to find himself he must place himself at the disposal of others, he must love his fellowmen.

The word 'love' sums all this up, even if it is often used in superficial ways; so we need to contemplate the Christ who shows us how God loves, how Jesus loves, how he becomes a servant, laying aside the power which is his by right. "Having the power of God within him, he humbled himself" (Philippians 2:5).

In our own lives, we should set ourselves consciously to serve others and be at their disposal. In the Church, we should be ready for persecution and martyrdom. The Church shows such readiness when, in the face of opposition, she humbly preaches the Word and goes on, up to a point, in silence, in order to continue her witness to the truth, thus fulfilling her supreme service to mankind.

Only the Holy Spirit, entering our hearts as the gift of the Risen Lord, will enable us, day by day, to make the Gospel a real part of our lives, the Gospel which reveals the being of God, the reality of God in Jesus and Jesus in us. Nevertheless, the contemplation of Christ crucified is a source of great enlightenment for us and for the Church as she seeks to serve the world.

Jesus evangelist

The last scene, which follows immediately, is that in which Jesus shows himself fully as an evangelist and reaps the first fruits of his life and death as an evangelist. "One of the criminals hanging on the cross insulted him: You are the Christ, aren't you? Save yourself and us. But the other rebuked him: Aren't you afraid of God even though you have received the same sentence? We were justly condemned and are getting the due reward of our deeds, but this man has done nothing wrong. And he added: Jesus, remember me when you come into your Kingdom. He answered: Truly I tell you, today you will be with me in Paradise" (Luke 23:39-43).

Let us pause for a moment over these words, recorded

by St Luke alone; they are a penetrating analysis of the gradual growth of a convert.

At the same time, let us think what sort of a man he was: a criminal, one who had lived a life of violence, by the tyranny of the strongest and who, at a certain point, had had to succumb to others stronger than himself. Now he finds himself in a situation where he could have felt a supreme loathing, rage and anger against society; certainly it was a position of extreme confusion and misery. Instead, when he sees Jesus suffering humbly and gently, he gradually comes to realize that new values and relationships are possible — there is not only violence and the tyranny of the strong. He discovers a sort of person which he had never known before, whose existence he did not even suspect — he is there, next to him. He discovers a new type of man who does not play the strong man's game, who does not avail himself of his own power (that power which others at least attribute to him), who yields himself to his own suffering.

It is truly something incredible, unheard-of, which gradually brings him to an understanding of this Nazarene who has made himself one with the guilty: "We were justly condemned for our deeds, but this man has done nothing wrong". He begins to see connections between things and to assess people accurately and the essential goodness, which he certainly possessed, surfaces gradually and is given free expression; there is a difference between us and him, he represents a different type of human being.

Up to this point it is only his human goodness which has surfaced; but there comes a moment when, seeing the way Jesus suffers and abandons himself into the Father's hands, he takes the decisive step of faith expressed in this prayer: "Jesus, remember me when you come into your Kingdom".

Note that this is the first time in the Gospel when Jesus is called so familiarly by his name. (The apostles call him 'Lord' or 'Master'.) Here the fellowship of suffering has led rapidly to the friendship of deep mutual understanding: he senses a friend in Jesus, he feels perfectly understood and knows that he can address him by his first name: "Jesus, remember me when you come into your Kingdom". Thus he expresses his friendship, faith and surrender to the power of God at work in Jesus; he is a man who has perfectly understood the Gospel, he has understood that in this crucified man God's power is made manifest and a way of life, quite different from his own, has been shown to him; it is a way of brotherly love which he himself can put into action at this very moment by a word of friendship. If we are friends, we can trust each other and if this friend is powerful he can help me, I can rely on him.

Here is a man who, in a few moments, has reshaped the pattern of his relationships. He has passed from a life full of suspicion, violence and mutual wrongdoing to a situation of friendship, loyalty, trust, mutual surrender and openness. Behind all this is God, who, if he manifests himself at all, will do so in this new type of humanity — friendly, trustful, dignified in suffering, able to form new relationships. Then comes Jesus' reply: "Truly I tell you, today you will be with me in Paradise". He is the first person whom Jesus saves, the first to be evangelized. He is evangelized without the Resurrection, simply by the glory of God which shines through Jesus' acceptance of suffering and injustice.

These are things which we can hardly understand and which we find it difficult to put into words because we know very well that — as in the case of those tangible realities which convey life's deepest meaning — it is not so much a question of analyzing the words but of inner participation in Jesus' life: that is how we shall penetrate their true meaning.

Let us ask the Lord to help us to grasp these lessons of evangelical power which the Passion of Jesus teaches us. These are lessons which are learned above all in prayer, lessons which the Church continually brings before us as means of renewing the true Christian life of service and availability in a Church which can give birth to a new type of man — a man who bears witness, amid the sad story of cruelty and injustice, to the power and glory of God.

The salvation which Jesus offers from the Cross

We ask you, Lord, that our prayer may be a sharing with yours in the Garden of Gethsemane and on the Cross, with Mary's prayer at the foot of the Cross, with the prayer of the thief who turns to Jesus and sees his life saved by the mercy of God.

This prayer is not only for us but for the whole Church, for all those who put their trust in us and for all those who struggle to find in their own lives the signs of redemption. Help, sustain and enlighten us all; help us all to know — as did the thief on the cross — that we are loved, understood, forgiven; help us all to share in the mysterious maternity of Mary at the Cross. We ask this, Father, through Jesus Christ our Lord. Amen.

To further our understanding of the salvation Jesus offers us, let us continue to meditate on the Passion and the way in which it reveals to us the nature of God. Let us turn once more to the penitent thief and then to Mary at the foot of the Cross.

Our individual importance to God

Luke lays great stress on the episode of the *penitent, redeemed thief*, and he presents it as the culmination of Jesus' redemptive, evangelizing work in his Passion. If we judge this from a human viewpoint we cannot help asking: is that all? Just one man! So many of the people just went home, one or two of them a bit shaken but mostly without having understood the significance of the scene.

Why such a waste of evangelical power for such a very meagre result?

Let us look again at the episode of the redeemed thief in the light of a very important chapter in Luke (ch. 15):

"All the tax-collectors and sinners drew near to hear him. The Pharisees and scribes started to mutter: This man receives sinners and eats with them. And he told them this parable . . ." and three parables follow: the lost sheep, the lost coin and the lost son. These three parables are meant to be read together; they help us to understand the God of the Gospel, the God whom Jesus reveals in his forgiveness of the thief from the Cross.

First of all, we should note that all these parables are quite definitely concerned with the *one* rather than the many: one sheep, one coin, one son; in the case of the son it is obvious that only one of the two sons is important; in the case of the sheep (one out of a hundred) or in the case of the coin (one of a set of ten), we can see that the importance the parables give to the *one* is both enormous and exaggerated.

The parable of the lost sheep

"Which of you, having a hundred sheep and losing one of them, does not leave the ninety-nine in the desert and go looking for the lost one until he finds it?" (Luke 15:4). We would say: but why leave the ninety-nine in the desert to go in search of one? Besides, the text does not imply that the shepherd has left them well-guarded! The shepherd's behaviour seems a bit extreme, even slightly crazy: he puts the sheep over his shoulder and returns happily home, inviting all his friends and neighbours to celebrate with him. . . . All this seems to me to show us *how important each one of us is to God*, even just one, even the least of us. This does not tally, in fact it is in complete contrast with the pagan image of God who is certainly concerned with the world but does not love the individual.

The same emphases appear in the other two parables — the woman who carefully sweeps the house to find the coin and the prodigal son who returns to the father's house.

This gives us a new insight into the image of God which we find in the Cross, where Jesus saves a criminal and out-law, a wretched man, abandoned by all. This is the *trade-*

mark of God, the God of the Gospel: one, only one person is enough to justify all the divine care, attention — and joy. There is always an emphasis on the joy: the shepherd invites his friends to celebrate with him and "so there will be more joy in heaven over one converted sinner than over ninety-nine good people". The woman says "Share my joy", and "so I tell you, there is joy among the angels". The father says, "We must have a feast to celebrate". This is what the God of the Gospel is like. God has everything in hand, he is lord of all, he is the King who rules heaven and earth but he can deeply love just one person, he cannot rest even if there is just one soul in distress.

This same teaching can often be found in the sayings of Jesus: "Woe to you if you cause any of these little ones to sin"; "when you did it to *just one* of these, you did it to me". As the exegetes so rightly point out, the emphasis on 'just one' is a striking characteristic of the Gospel. God expresses his joy when even one person has been saved.

This point is important in the priestly ministry: priests certainly minister to all men, to the many, and have to care for a whole community, but only on certain special occasions do they enjoy the satisfaction of seeing the full fruition of their labours. Jesus' joy is a reflection of God's total caring for human beings, and before the whole world he declares the value of the person, even one person; so if one person is worth so much, many people are worth even more and no one can be neglected.

Let us ask God to help us to understand his merciful care which he communicates to us and which we in turn should convey to the community; it is this care which clearly differentiates Christian commitment from, say, politics or the social services; these, in the final analysis, treat the woes of the world without worrying overmuch if this or that individual is unwelcome or neglected.

It is true that this is but one aspect of the experience of God: the experience of God means, in fact, salvation for all men but fully to understand the God of the Gospel means to care for the salvation of all men in such a way that no single person is neglected, offended or forgotten; it means giving to each one the value which he has in the eyes of God.

The way of Mary

There is someone who experiences the full reality of redemption at the Cross and this is Mary. She is of priceless worth to Jesus who places his gifts of salvation in her and sees in her, in the name of the Church, the first complete human response to his boundless love.

As we look at Mary at the foot of the Cross we should try to understand what happened to her at that moment, and how God had gradually led her to the point of being able to identify herself with the redemption wrought on that Cross. Taking as our starting point a passage from *Lumen Gentium* which says that "Mary went from strength to strength in the pilgrimage of faith", we can look back from the scene of Mary at the Cross and pick out some of the stages in her life which will show us how God prepared her.

The start of Mary's pilgrimage can be found in Luke's Gospel in chapter 1 verse 29 when the angel comes to her and "at these words she was troubled". This is Mary's first encounter with the new world of God: the Greek word — *dietarachthe*, "she was troubled" — is a very strong word and it is surprising that Luke should have used it on this occasion. It is the same word used, for example, in Matthew 2:3, "Herod was troubled and all Jerusalem with him" (Herod was troubled at the news of the Magi); or in Luke 1:12, "Zechariah's heart was troubled" by the apparition of the angel; or again in Matthew 14:26 where we read that the disciples were troubled when Jesus walked on the water. So Mary, too, felt this initial agitation: where is God leading me, what is going to happen? Mary was certainly accustomed to a regular life of prayer, piety and religious commitment and to hearing the Word of God in the Bible, but now she senses that God is lifting her to a different plane and — like Abraham — she will have to leave her former securities behind her and yield herself to God in a new way.

G

This is where Mary starts learning about that divine plan which will be partly in keeping with, partly contrary to her expectations. Both these aspects are emphasized in the rest of Luke's Gospel whenever Mary is mentioned. Stress is laid on Mary's perfect conformity to God's will when she answers the angel (Luke 1 : 38) or when Elizabeth says to her: "How have I deserved to have the Mother of my Lord visit me?" Here we have a perfect response to God's plan, a certain enthusiasm and joy in what God has asked of her and is doing within her. Mary makes an initial response of enthusiasm to her calling, all seems set fair, as the Lord had shown her, so she accepts wholeheartedly God's plan for her life.

However, the Gospel records that very soon Mary enters what we might call the 'years of obscurity'. Luke stresses this on various occasions: during the visit to Jerusalem when she is told that a sword will pierce her heart, or when Jesus answers them in the Temple and she cannot understand what is happening: "When they saw him, they were astonished and his mother said to him: Son, why did you do this to us? See how your father and I have been desperately worried, looking for you" (Luke 2 : 48), and the Evangelist adds: "But they did not understand what he said to them". It is interesting to note that this phrase: "But they did not understand what he said to them" is the phrase which recurs in the predictions of the Passion when the apostles do not understand what Jesus says to them about the Cross and Resurrection: "They did not understand what was said to them and these words were obscure to them" (Luke 18 : 34). So Mary also *shares this same obscurity*; she understands and yet she fails to understand God's plan, she follows it entirely, embracing it wholeheartedly (she always adheres to it with a perfect and faultless faith) but she has to accept that God's plan is different from what she, as a mother, could ever have imagined; obviously a mother desires for her son a plan which involves a successful outcome, certain visible results.

A gradual expropriation takes place in Mary's heart — every mother wants to possess her own son, or rather is tempted to be possessive and to make him realize her own ambitions for him.

In Jesus' public life there are clear indications whereby the Master affirms his freedom to carry out his own plans in the face of any parental plans for him (even hypothetical ones). When, for example, his relations come and he does not even want to receive them or when he is praised: "Blessed is the womb which carried you and the breast which fed you", he replies, "Blessed rather are those who hear the word of God" (Luke 11:27-28).

Mary's blessedness, therefore, lies in total conformity to the divine plan. We certainly cannot think that Jesus lacked love for his mother: if Jesus feels the tears of the woman who has lost her son (Luke 7:13), he must love his own mother dearly but *just because he loves her*, he gives first place to his freedom for messianic action, trusting that Mary will totally accept God's action in her own life.

It is difficult for us to enter into the path which Mary had to tread and we can only appreciate it fully when we meditate on the words of her Son from the Cross: then we shall understand how far his mother had come. She followed him right to the Cross — Luke himself tells us this — and John gives us the whole scene, recording the words which Jesus spoke to her.

Let us try to identify ourselves with Mary, in prayer and silent adoration of the crucified Lord, asking ourselves what took place at that moment in Mary's soul, what would have been her wish as a mother. It is probably true to say that, as a mother, she would have wished to give her own life, and to stop this happening at any cost; instead the Lord teaches her to accept in a mysterious and profound way the divine plan whereby it is Jesus, the Saviour, who represents the perfection of the Father's love.

This is the most dramatic moment of Mary's life, when she really gives up her Son to the Father on behalf of humanity; and at that moment she receives from the Son the whole of humanity. This is the main point made by John who, in the person of the disciple, presents the Church to us, the Church which is placed in close communion with the Lord's mother as a result of the Passion in which Mary shared with Jesus.

What then does Our Lady represent as she stands at the summit of her way of faithful conformity to the will of God? She represents humanity, the Church. Having followed God's will completely, having embraced it whole-heartedly, having offered up her Son in faith — as Abraham was called to do — she receives, as a gift, the very fullness of the Church. Precisely because she has put her whole self in God's hands and has abandoned herself along with all she held most dear, her own Son, she receives from God what he holds most dear, the body of the Son which will live in the Church, that Church which is to be born from the Passion, Death and Resurrection of Jesus. Mary is the one who, more than anyone else, understood the meaning of Jesus' sacrificial offering, the love of humanity and the total dedication to God's plan which this offering implies; she is above all others fitted to receive from God the gift of renewed humanity.

It is on this that we must base our love for the Lord's mother. If we lose sight of Mary's journey of faith, we shall no longer be able to understand how God has actually saved us, giving us, in Jesus, to Mary, so that in her the Church might come into being.

Obviously we can approach these truths in many ways; by way of popular Christian devotion, in sensational or in unobtrusive manner. Every time the Church becomes freshly aware of Mary's presence, there is a new burst of Christian life, with its accompanying strength, serenity, gracefulness and vivacity, precisely because we are taken back to the fundamental mysteries of the redemption. This is neither a luxury nor an optional extra: it is a question of placing ourselves at the foot of the Cross and understanding how humanity enters into God's plan, accepts redemption and, in Mary, starts out on the road to salvation.

Let us ask the Lord to help us truly to understand the mysteries of God in our lives: either by means of the rosary or other forms of Marian devotion that we can identify with and help others to do the same, or by simply contemplating the mysteries of Mary in the Gospel: whatever we do it is certain that the presence of the Virgin exercises a mysterious and salutary influence which helps us to enter into the meaning of redemption.

Let us also ask that we may help Christian people, who are so aware of these realities, to live them in a way that is upright, efficacious and true. It is good to find that people still feel and express a great love for Our Lady: let us use this love to urge folk to follow the way Mary went, clinging wholeheartedly to the mystery of God, to his will; this is a way of great spiritual fruitfulness and has brought many into the Church; thus Jesus' redemptive work on the Cross, accomplished for the few and with such apparently meagre results, has been richly multiplied.

If we entrust the results of Jesus' redemptive action to Mary, many are brought into the Church, as the Acts of the Apostles bear witness.

Let us persevere in this prayer at the foot of the Cross, in company with the Virgin.

The words of the risen Lord

We thank you, Lord, that you appeared in your risen body to Peter and the apostles and disciples and charged them afresh with the mission of evangelization and pastoral care.

We thank you that you sent your Spirit upon them, filling them with the assurance of your living presence, putting the right words into their mouths and guiding them in times of joy and hardship. We ask you, Lord, to show yourself in our midst as you showed yourself to your apostles; we ask you to show yourself in our midst with your Spirit as you showed yourself in the Cenacle to the apostles, gathered together with Mary.

Put your words on our lips, inspire us with your intentions and help us to share anew in your mission.

Help us to leave this place with a fresh awareness of the gift of Christian witness which you in your mercy have placed in our hearts that many others may be drawn to you.

We ask this of you, Lord, who live and reign with the Father and the Holy Spirit throughout the ages. Amen.

These are the words of the risen Lord to the Twelve, as recorded at the end of Luke's Gospel (ch. 24) or at the beginning of Acts: "You will be given power by the Holy Spirit who will come down on you and you will witness to me in Jerusalem, in all Judaea and Samaria and to the ends of the earth" (Acts 1 : 8).

Let us ask three things concerning these words: firstly, in what state of mind Peter and the other apostles receive the words of the risen Christ; secondly, what are these words and their meaning? thirdly, in what situations do we receive them and what do they have to say to us today?

What stage have they reached in their formation as evangelists? Here it is useful to sum up the various aspects of the journey taken by the apostles as they followed Jesus, looking at Peter in particular.

These men were in some sense witnesses of the Master's first apostolic defeat at Nazareth where Jesus is rejected and goes away outwardly beaten but free in spirit for he knows that this is his Father's work, not his own.

Then comes Peter's miraculous catch of fish when Peter, recognizing his own poverty and frailty beside the power at work in Jesus, sets himself enthusiastically to follow the Lord. Successive enthusiasms follow: association with the Master who attracts crowds of people, works miracles and heals the sick; association with Jesus' work, with the sufferings of the people, with the faith ministries to which the apostles are called and which they exercise; as they become aware of the great misery and suffering in the world, they also become aware, especially Peter, of their responsibility; Peter ponders on his own mission until he thinks of it as something personal, almost a privilege, something for which he is directly responsible.

Then comes the second part of Luke's Gospel in which Jesus trains the apostles in detachment, abandonment to the Father, teaching them that all they possess, including their evangelical mission itself, is the result of the Father's work in them. Finally comes the hard lesson of the Passion and death: Peter learns that salvation comes from the Lord alone and that he himself is the first to benefit from this work of salvation. Like Mary, Peter finds that what he thought was his own role, is taken away from him only to be mercifully restored to him by the Lord in the form of God's work within him: that is the moment when Peter and the apostles receive their commission to humanity.

In order to review one of the important aspects of the apostles' training period as evangelists, let us look again at the text with which we started, which speaks of the unity of the body and the gifts which Jesus gives to the Church:

"There is one body, one spirit, as there is one hope to which you have been called; one Lord, one faith, one baptism, one God, Father of all, who is above all, works through all things and is present in you all" (Ephesians 4: 4-6).

So *this* is the work which God accomplishes in the world; this is the work of salvation which is not ours and is not assigned to us; God himself, in a mysterious way, is carrying forward this work in all things and in all men.

Paul goes on to say: "But to each one of you grace is given according to the measure of the gift of Christ". And: "It is he who has made some men apostles, others prophets, others evangelists, others pastors and teachers, to fit the brothers to fulfil the ministry and finally to build up the Body of Christ" (Ephesians 4: 7 ff.).

It is the Father's work, it is the work which Jesus accomplished on the Cross, the work of the infinite love of the Father which — through Christ — is poured out on each one of us; it is given to us as a grace, a gift, a sharing in this work, according to the measure Christ gives; and as long as it continues to spring up freshly and freely within us — not as a source of heaviness, sadness or bitterness but as a source of enthusiasm and originality — we shall retain the grace and gift which the risen Lord continually gives us.

To be evangelists, pastors and priests is a gift of God, and in order to fulfil our vocation as a gift, in order to have liberty, joy and calm detachment from immediate results, we must not slow down — that would be the exact opposite of what the Lord wants! — rather we must make a real effort to rethink and reassess our position, to look at it afresh from time to time, to ask ourselves the meaning of what we are doing, why we are doing it and how we could do it better.

At the time of their commission to preach the Gospel, the apostles had realized that the divine mandate was not to be received as a burdensome possession to be jealously guarded and managed in a private and personal way; rather, it was a gift from the risen Lord, a gift which was given to them at the moment when they were no longer expecting it, when they feared that the Lord had abandoned them because of their unfaithfulness. Instead, the Lord, the great

96

Evangelist and herald of God's mercy, places this treasure of ministry in their hands because he has confidence in them and entrusts it to their open hearts.

The fact that they had arrived at this stage in their evangelical training, explains the Gospel joy, the liberty, originality and unperturbable serenity which can be found on every page of the Acts of the Apostles. One example will suffice — Acts 5 : 41, where we read that the apostles, having been beaten, flogged and driven out: "went away happy to have been insulted for the love of the Name".

Their joy and serenity in spite of the blows they had received, show us how fully they accepted the gift as God's, not theirs, in the certainty that, somehow or other, God himself was working through them.

Let us ask God to keep us always in his grace and to help us to understand that the ministry with all its wearisome labour, its hardships and difficulties, is given to us *as a gift* and is not meant to oppress us with worry and sorrow, although we may indeed have to face such things because we share in the worries, sorrows, sufferings and death of the people to whom we minister. We are constantly in contact with cases of extreme human suffering, but the Gospel and the ability to evangelize is still given to us as a gift, a free grace. Paul repeats in his letters: "We have been given this gift, this ability; of ourselves we are incapable of doing or saying anything and our capacity comes from God, it is his gift which enables us to do, to speak and to act".

"My witnesses"

What are the words spoken to the apostles in the divine commission at the beginning of Acts?: "You will receive power from the Holy Spirit who will come down on you and you will be witnesses to me in Jerusalem, in all Judaea and Samaria and to the very ends of the earth" (Acts 1 : 8).

Let us begin with the central affirmation: "You will be witnesses to me".

So the apostles are called to be witnesses: *who is a*

97

witness? Someone who has seen something and swears to what he has seen. But in the language of Acts it is something more, it is *someone who is personally committed to what he has seen and understood* — as in a court of law one witnesses in someone's defence.

What do they witness to? They are witnesses *to me.* The testimony of the apostles concerns the person of Jesus, his power, his life, his ability to renew mankind, to give new hope to the thief on the cross who was on the brink of despair, to build new relationships based on service and friendship freely offered; it is always to Jesus that they are witnesses, rather than to a plan, an idea or a project.

How do they bear witness? The same verse 8 tells us: "You will receive power when the Holy Spirit comes down on you". Jesus knows very well that the Church has a long way to travel and will need not only her memory of the past but also an experience and gift in the present: this is the *gift of the Holy Spirit* without which it is impossible to accomplish the work of evangelism. It is the power of the Spirit which we received in the laying-on of hands, and which is continually given afresh in prayer and the celebration of the Eucharist. Every time we invoke him, the Spirit gives us this power, he inspires our evangelical activity and helps us to experience afresh the grace of our ordination.

Here we can develop what we might call a *priestly ascesis*, the austerity of life which gives priority to private prayer and meditation, communal prayer and prayer for our own ministry, also a careful celebration of the Eucharist with due preparation and an effort to make it central to the day.

The power of the Spirit is described in the New Testament as the power which gives love, joy, peace, serenity and trust; when we feel we are lacking any of these things, it means that we have to make fresh contact with this power for without it the memorial of Christ becomes just words and these words which we repeat seem unable to help us.

In our time the Church is continually rediscovering the presence of the Spirit which finds expression in vital Christian experience.

Jesus puts the two things together: "You will receive

power from the Spirit" and "you will witness to me". The one does not happen without the other: and, for our own sake as well as for others, we should often make room for the Spirit of God to enter our lives, giving his power full freedom of action within us.

"You will witness to me in Jerusalem, in Judaea, in Samaria and to the ends of the earth." Obviously these words have a geographical significance and refer to the spread of the Gospel in Acts, but they also have a philological meaning. That is, this gift is not for you only, for a small group of a few initiates; *it is a gift for everyone* "to the ends of the earth". Be sure that you will not be sent into any human situation where there is not a profound thirst for truth, justice and brotherhood and therefore, at bottom a profound thirst for God.

This makes us think — as we look around us and see so many people, caught in the anonymity of city life (in the underground especially, or at the station) — of the way in which God can manifest himself in this city, to these people.

While we feel our hearts contracting slightly in fear, the Lord answers us, as he did Paul at Corinth: "Do not be afraid, for there are many people who are *for me* in this city" (Acts 18:9, 10). God will provide his own ways of helping those people; at the moment, perhaps, not all of them are ready to come straight into the Church in the strict sense, but we can say with certainty that there are people on the Lord's side in this city; there is a certain uneasiness, an expectation and *we are sent to meet this expectation,* we and others — the Lord works in many ways — and he will go to prepare the way for us.

If we apply ourselves to the task, we can discover his will and help him, even if we do only a little; and if we cannot lead many people the whole way, we may nevertheless be able to give a word of hope and throw a bit of light in their path and then others will do the rest. Jesus says in John 4:38: "Others have laboured and you have come into their labours"; we are not always assured of completing the building from start to finish, and often our contribution will be merely a bit of help, perhaps important and decisive, but still incomplete.

"You will witness to me — to the ends of the earth". There are three important ways in which we carry forward the evangelical mission entrusted to the Twelve. We do this *in the faith of Peter and the Church, with the witness of the Spirit, and by means of opening up the Scriptures.*

In the faith of Peter. We are not among those who have seen and welcomed the risen Lord; we are among those who believed and who started the chain of believers which stretches down as far as us.

Our Christian life, our preaching and priesthood is founded *on the apostles, on the living tradition, on the magisterium* which comes down from the apostles right to John Paul II; it is rooted in the Church which Christ promised us would never fail. We live and act *at all times* sustained by the Church and her tradition, her life and her hierarchy; if we separate ourselves, even slightly, from this body, we no longer amount to anything, as history bears witness. Think of all the individuals or groups who thought they could accomplish something in opposition to the Church, who had extraordinary projects in mind and then realized that in the measure that they departed from the visible Church, the apostolic tradition and the Popes, they lost their impact on society as well as their strength and effectiveness.

So with all their criticisms of the institutional Church, with all the ideas they proposed — even good and worthwhile ones — inasmuch as they separated themselves from this matrix, they lost their apostolic drive, power and impact. This is the law which shows us that — even if we do not realize it — our activity is at all times strictly bound to the Church and to the mainstream of tradition. Actually it happens that many problems are quite simply beyond us; there is plenty we cannot understand or explain on our own and we need to lean on the Church, on those who have gone before us and who will follow us; we must rely on the faith of the Saints and on the anonymous sanctity of all those who, over the centuries, have carried the torch of faith. This is that anonymous sanctity which has brought us in touch with the supernatural: the mothers, the parents of priests, the priests who taught us, those parish priests from whom we learned the true meaning of life. *All this is the Church* on which we lean, in whose name we preach, with whom we proclaim the Resurrection. During the Easter ceremonies, when we proclaim that Christ is risen, it is not we, not our voice alone which speaks out in the Church, but the voice of the whole Church, which we interpret.

We seek God, we have a deep desire for him as St Augustine says. We would like to see and taste him but we understand that we cannot go to him unless we go together, each relying on the faith of the others, on others' abilities, intelligence and clarity of vision. This is what the human condition involves: not a presumptuous attempt to solve all life's problems on our own but a realization that we are called to solve them together.

The catholic Church also expresses this profound truth: *we go to God together*, not only in the present and past but also in the future. In the future the Church will understand the things we do not understand today, she will be more fully aware of the universal implications of Christ's saving work. We should rejoice in this future capacity of the Church even if at present we suffer because some things remain unexplained, some questions are still unsettled; perhaps it seems to us that there are areas of human experience to which the Church has given insufficient value and attention. We are on the road, and we can rejoice in the possibilities which will open up to the Church in the future.

Vatican II made it clear that, until the end of time, the Church will go on increasing in the knowledge of God and the faith. We represent but one stage on the journey of endless development which the Lord gives to his Church; our hearts reach out in hope to the future, we do not pretend to have achieved all possible good already. It is an historic way that we tread and we must respect its laws, knowing that we are simply a tiny part of it, we are mere drops of water in a huge river flowing towards God. So it is in the power of Peter and the tradition of the Church that we live, preach, work and bear witness.

With the witness of the Spirit. I am always struck here by the phrase from Acts which explains and clarifies what we have said: "You will receive power from the Spirit" (Acts 1:8). And, even better, Peter before the Sanhedrin explains the meaning and source of his witness: "We are witnesses of these things, as is the Holy Spirit whom God has given to those who obey him" (Acts 5:32). So we are not only witnesses who, on the basis of the apostolic witness, continue to proclaim the message, but we can also say: see the works of the Spirit in the Church.

What are those works? They are the works of faith, hope and charity which give life to the Church and which are evident to anyone without prejudice. It is true that the prejudiced can always find fault and can always point to some area in the world which is unsatisfactory but when an unprejudiced person really encounters acts of faith, love and sacrifice (even of life itself), acts of consistent and persevering unselfishness, then he cannot help saying: here is something that I cannot explain, something which goes beyond the merely utilitarian, something which cannot be understood in terms of ordinary, everyday life.

The Church is alive and remains alive only insofar as she inspires continual acts of charity, selfless service, courage in the face of trials, cheerful acceptance of suffering and death, all of which things provide a double witness, that is, they bear out in our lives the witness of our lips. Moreover, what is it that attracts the young? They are attracted precisely by serenity, joy and unselfishness and the spirit of sacrifice. They understand that there is something there and they try to find out what it is; they discover what it is by means of the *kerygma* which we preach and to which both the Spirit and our truly Christian lives bear witness.

The opening up of the Scriptures. The two disciples of Emmaus do not say: "He explained the Scriptures to us" but "he opened up the Scriptures to us". There are two words used. In Luke 24:27 it says that, starting with Moses and all the prophets, Jesus explained to them all the things concerning him and in verse 32 it says: "Didn't our hearts burn within us while he spoke to us on the way and opened up the Scriptures to us?" The text is very precise. We translate simply: "Didn't our hearts burn within us?" but the Greek has a present participle: "Wasn't our heart gradually catching fire while he spoke like that and opened up the Scriptures?"

What does it mean to "open up the Scriptures"? It means putting the events of salvation — at which the disciples had been present without grasping their meaning — into the general context of salvation history which will make their meaning clear. This is the value of opening up the Scriptures. The Scriptures present us with God's plan for man in history, the gradual development of man's understanding of God, and the way of justice, truth and brotherhood. Jesus is presented as the culmination of this way and his Resurrection as the key to the whole plan, the explanation of all man's desires and man's continual aspiration to eternal life, justice and truth — all man's deepest thoughts and desires are thus lifted up to the level of the Spirit of Truth and given their true significance.

So in Scripture we find a way of drawing the divinely inspired threads of human desire for truth and goodness into a coherent whole in which the Resurrection is seen as the seal of God on a plan of salvation and not as a strange and unexpected event. I feel that the Scriptures both understand and interpret me, the Scriptures tell me what I desire and fear and give me the key to both aspirations and expectations. They provide a mirror for the man who is seeking God, the man who is searching for truth and the meaning of life, trying to escape the despair and fear which grip him when he finds himself without ideals and throws himself into experiences which either excite or numb him for a while only to let him fall once more into the void. The Scriptures reveal man to himself with his desires and his destiny, and help him to understand how the preaching of the risen Lord is indeed God's seal on all he has been doing in the history of the world's salvation.

These are the treasures which have been entrusted to us: the Church, her witness, her preaching, her *magisterium,* the Spirit who, in us and in others, fills life with joy, and the Scriptures — these last being extended by the commentaries of the Fathers, theology and the *magisterium* which explains and amplifies them. *And it is a gift,* we must remember, it is not a burden, nor is it some huge citadel which is difficult to maintain on account of its complexity; it is a gift, it is *the* gift of God, it is *Jesus himself* given to us quite simply as a gift and therefore immediately perceptible to the man of good will; it is, however, a gift which has to be explained, amplified, specified, extended into a way of faith; it must be expressed in a pastoral programme which embraces different times and places and situations, varying activities, wishes and events. We must always start from this fundamental unity which is the gift of grace, of salvation. It is a gift which fills the heart with joy, illuminating everything else with the light that is the evangelical gift of God.

Let us ask the Lord so to unify our lives that we may attend with undivided hearts to the various complexities of our day and the different types of service that our ministry involves.

May the Holy Spirit grant us that unity of life which simplifies everything — as we read in the lives of the Saints — makes everything clear and easy; so let us come back to him whenever our ministry is burdensome or tiring, for in this original simplicity is the solution we seek and the gift for which we so ardently long.